The Sweet Spot

MICHAEL CHILES

First published 2021

by John Catt Educational Ltd,
15 Riduna Park, Station Road,
Melton, Woodbridge IP12 1QT

Tel: +44 (0) 1394 389850
Fax: +44 (0) 1394 386893
Email: enquiries@johncatt.com
Website: www.johncatt.com

© 2021 Michael Chiles

Illustrations by David Goodwin

ISBN: 978 1 913622 56 5

Set and designed by John Catt Educational Limited

PRAISE FOR THE SWEET SPOT

The Sweet Spot illustrates collective practical wisdom alongside pedagogical theory. Chiles draws together knowledge about how classrooms and teachers can be as effective as possible. He illustrates the importance of subject knowledge combined with the benefits of clarity and simplicity, whilst also encouraging the reader to build trust through an authentic style that insists on high challenge. Highly recommended.

Alison Peacock CEO of Chartered College of Teaching, teacher, author, professor, Hon Fellow Queen's Cambridge, Hon Fellow UCL

The Sweet Spot provides a detailed examination of the elements which enable us to find the perfect balance in our classroom to optimise learning. Michael Chiles pays close attention to some of the key levers which will allow us to make some incremental, and some not so incremental, changes to our classroom practices.

The Sweet Spot begins by considering how we can optimise the learning experience, by looking at the conditions for learning, including classroom layout and aesthetics, before moving on to the topics of subject content, curriculum, and the quality of explanation. Chiles provides reflections on his own experiences throughout and deftly weaves through the research which underpins this. There are also many opportunities provided for readers to actively reflect on their own practices and how they might adapt them. This is a practical book as well as a thought-provoking read. The case studies illustrate the topics covered from a variety of perspectives and includes Kate Jones looking at modelling, Richard Clutterbuck who explores religious studies and Emma Turner providing a primary perspective.

The practical aspect of the book is further reinforced by the addition of resources and exemplars to support the reader to examine how they might put these ideas into action, making sure the art of teaching continues to be refined.

The book is a really important resource for those new to the classroom as well as those who are still keen to get involved in the discussion around what hitting the 'sweet spot' in teaching really means.

Zoe Enser, author, ex-head of department, teacher and T&L/CPD lead, English adviser and ELE, working with TDT

What are the key factors that influence explanation and modelling in the classroom? Michael digs into this essential 'nuts and bolts' issue, grapples with the evidence, and provides a range of practitioner case studies, all in a highly readable manner.

Peps Mccrea, Dean at Ambition Institute and author of the High Impact Teaching series

In an age where teachers are becoming more aware of the cognitive science behind the likes of cognitive load theory and dual-coding, *The Sweet Spot* offers a timely resource on explaining and modelling in the classroom. I found the content around designing PowerPoint slides fascinating as this is such an integral (and often time-heavy) part of teaching. With many pauses along the way for self-reflection, I think anyone interested in scaffolding, explaining, modelling and supporting their students to process information will very much enjoy this book. I strongly recommend it!

The Sweet Spot is an insightful and engaging read which should be found in CPD libraries in staffrooms everywhere. Underpinned by the latest research, Michael Chiles draws on his own wealth of expertise and experience, encouraging readers to reflect on their practice in order to provide an optimum learning experience for children and young people. Chiles champions the importance of teacher subject knowledge and curriculum content whilst encouraging educators to consider the best use of their time, from classroom set up to providing expert explanation and modelling, a careful balance of pedagogical theory and practical advice is needed in order to maximise learning opportunities and outcomes for learners. This is the book many of us will wish we had read at the start of our careers. It is an honest, thought-provoking and highly relevant read which all readers will be able to relate to and take something away from.

Sarah Mullin, deputy headteacher, doctoral research student and author of *What They Didn't Teach Me on My PGCE* and *Chronicles from the Classroom*

This is the kind of book that every teacher needs in their life. Michael Chiles has created a blueprint for how to excel at explaining and modelling. *The Sweet Spot* is a fascinating yet straightforward read. It has a user-friendly structure, perfect for expert and novice alike. Chiles explores the key principles for explaining and modelling by setting each of them out in clear terms, looking at what the research says and then giving practical advice on what the reader should do. We particularly liked the analytical way the use of analogies was explored by Chiles, breaking them down into clear steps, complete with visuals to ensure a really grounded understanding for the reader. There were many points where we followed up on the research mentioned by Chiles in the book that have helped us to further develop our own understanding of key pedagogical concepts. In short, it is an excellent read, highly recommended.

Jane Miller and Finola Wilson, Impact Wales

For Ralph Gilbert,
forever in my heart.

CONTENTS

FOREWORD BY JOHN TOMSETT

When a cricketer plays what looks like a forward defensive but the ball hurtles unstoppably towards the boundary, they have hit the ball out of the *sweet spot* – the very centre – of the bat. The shot will be perfectly timed, with the player's every sinew aligned to deliver the bat perfectly to the ball at precisely the right moment. It looks effortless but is the fruit of endless hours of practice under the tutelage of an expert coach who knows both the theory and the practice of sweet spot batting.

And so it is with *The Sweet Spot*, a book that brims with Michael's hard-earned teaching wisdom, underpinned by exhaustive, apposite research evidence. It is a truly accessible book that brings together, in one short tract, all you need to know about what the evidence says are the prerequisites for expert explanations and modelling. It is a book which epitomises Ben Goldacre's maxim: 'Being a good teacher isn't about robotically following the numerical output of randomised trials; nor is it about ignoring the evidence, and following your hunches and personal experiences instead. We do best, by using the right combination of skills to get the best job done.'[1]

The Sweet Spot is a book for our time. It complements the Early Career Framework brilliantly and yet it is a reminder for teachers of all ages and experience of the active ingredients of solidly good explanation and modelling. Nothing is left to chance. This book sweats the detail and Michael is not afraid to get stuck into the prosaic – but also essential – aspects of setting up your classroom in a way that maximises learning. Indeed, to use another metaphor, this gem of a book is like Dr Who's *Tardis* – its modest physical dimensions belie the breadth and depth of evidence-informed, common sense advice between its covers.

Without being explicit, what Michael does in this book is highlight what Dylan Wiliam considers the most important concept for all teachers: *opportunity cost*.

---

1. Goldacre, B. (2013) 'Building evidence into education'. Retrieved from: www.bit.ly/3gs7yK7

When you spend time on something – *anything* – that is time you cannot spend on something else. The author repeatedly answers this question: What is the most time efficient, effective way of explaining and modelling your subject to your pupils? Too often we spend time preparing teaching materials that look pretty but add nothing to their impact upon pupils' learning. Michael shows how important it is for teachers to spend their precious time preparing whatever it is that has the best chance possible of maximising pupils' progress.

What is endearing about Michael's style is his reflective honesty. He has made mistakes in the past and is open enough to admit them and explain how he consequently altered his teaching. Post-pandemic the *PowerPoint* presentation has regained some of its credibility and Michael outlines how to make best use of this ubiquitous teaching tool, after wasting too much time in the past making his slides look aesthetically pleasing but largely impact-free when it comes to helping pupils learn.

This book has made me think again about my own practice. I thought I could model writing for pupils, but the chapter entitled *The Classroom Toolkit* has given me a comprehensive range of different techniques for modelling and explaining my subject that goes beyond anything I had practised. And therein lies another important feature of this book: Michael unpicks the relationship between pedagogy and curriculum content. Here is a man who knows that you cannot teach something so that students know and understand it, if you do not know and understand it yourself. As Lawrence Stenhouse once wrote, 'curriculum development is teacher development'[2].

Michael concludes the book with contributions from his Sweet Spot Academy: some of the profession's rising stars, practitioners who share his attention to detail, sense of humility and understated expertise. *The Sweet Spot* is worth reading just for Emma Turner's entry alone: her advice on how to teach the fundamentals of fractions to the early years is both illuminating and delightful.

When you hit the cricket ball out of the sweet spot, batting feels like the easiest thing to do in the world. Now, the complexity of teaching 32 pupils in a cramped classroom on a wet and windy Thursday afternoon in late November is way beyond what it takes to send a ball to the boundary. That said, if you approach this book with the openness and humility of its author, I am sure the professional learning that you glean will help you find your own pedagogic *sweet spot*.

---

2. Stenhouse, L. (1975) *An introduction to curriculum research and development*. Pearson Education.

INTRODUCTION THE ART OF TEACHING

'If you can't explain it simply, you don't understand it well enough.' - Albert Einstein

Dominic Walliman once said, 'you can pretty much explain anything to anybody, as long as you go about it the right way'.[1] Right from the early dawn of time, humanity has been finding ways to communicate. Every day we are discovering new products and resources and then looking to explain these new discoveries. How these explanations are crafted will determine the recipient's understanding and, in turn, how this understanding mutates.

Picture this, a friend asks you about something you are knowledgeable about, you've been waiting for years for them to be interested. This is your moment to share what you know but you get carried away with your enthusiasm and you end up losing them in the conversation. In early childhood, children want to know 'stuff': 'Why is the sky blue?', 'How easy is it to drive?' As they start to speak, they want to know all about their surroundings, asking lots of whys and hows. There might be times where we decide to not fully explain the truth to one of those questions that a child asks. This inevitably leads to a point in time when we have to clarify and undo what we had previously told them. Whether we are explaining and modelling to children from an early age, or to our friends who show an interest in something we are knowledgeable about, the quality of our explanations is crucial.

Returning to our own classrooms, I'm sure we have all been there before when pupils have that light bulb moment, 'Ah, I get it now!' Or, on the other side of the spectrum, 'I don't get it!' Where pupils respond on this spectrum all depends on explanation and modelling forms a key pedagogy principle in our classroom.

---

1. Tedx Talks (2016, 24 May) *Quantum Physics for 7 Year Olds | Dominic Walliman | TEDxEastVan.* [Video] YouTube. Retrieved from: www.bit.ly/3xtY3zN

It's something we do every lesson, every day. When we explain in the classroom, we do so to enable pupils to acquire new knowledge and skills. Whilst when we model, we shine a light on how to apply the newly acquired knowledge and skills. Therefore, investing time into how we craft our explanations and models in our subject disciplines will influence the learning process.

In the chapters that follow, I will set out a series of key principles for explaining and modelling with precision and sharing a range of strategies on how we can do this in our classrooms.

In chapter 1, I will outline the role streamlining our classrooms can have in creating the foundations for our explanations. We will look at the research that underpins the core principles for setting up our pitch and then a series of recommendations. Chapter 2 will focus on preparing our explanations and models to ensure they are precise, unpicking the role of subject knowledge in crafting your explanations and we can ensure this part of our teacher armoury remains at the forefront of everything we do throughout our career.

In chapter 3, the focus shifts to how we deliver our explanations and models – the most pinnacle part of the key principles I outline in this book. This can be the make or break for a pupil's understanding and for teachers maximising the time we have with our pupils. Chapter 4 provides a classroom toolkit you can use to try out new approaches to explaining and modelling in your classroom, considering them from different subject lenses and how they might work to aid your teaching. In the final chapter, I'm joined by a fabulous group of colleagues who have taken the time to share how they explain and model a concept in their subject.

I hope you find this book helpful for your own classroom practice, as well as supporting others in developing their pedagogy. Ultimately, this is by no means a one size fits all approach to how we can explain and model with precision. But, based on reading the research, talking to teachers and reflecting on my own practice, I've shared a set of principles that I believe will support any teacher to find the sweet spot for two important components of teaching.

Introducing Sam

Sam, a teacher of fourteen years, is always reflecting on his teaching and still considers how to improve the learning experience his pupils receive. In this book, after taking into account the research, he will provide a series of recommendations for how you can put into practice the key principles and to find the 'sweet spot' to delivering explanations and models with precision.

1

THE STREAMLINED CLASSROOM

> **'Everything should be made as simple as possible, but not simpler.'** – Albert Einstein

It's September and the start of a new academic year. Sam is now in his third year of teaching and always enjoys the first few days of INSET because he knows there will be some time to get prepared for the first weeks back. On his to-do list is preparing his classroom for the new school year, including updating his displays, organising and re-labelling the boxes with his new teaching groups for their exercise books, and contemplating whether he should rearrange the table layout. For the third year in a row, he ponders whether it would be more beneficial to change from his tables of rows to a horseshoe arrangement or groups of tables.

1.1 The classroom layout

In the first few years of teaching, I remember being a lot like Sam and spending several hours during INSET days contemplating how to arrange my table layout. My consideration about the classroom layout was not influenced by my thought on how the arrangement would have an implication on learning, it was, in all honesty, just my desire for a change. My belief that the start of the new year symbolised a 'fresh start' and part of this required a change in the layout of the room. Equally, changing the layout would keep any previous pupils I taught last academic year on their toes when they arrived for the start of the new school year. One year I decided to go for the groups of tables. It seemed like a good idea, everyone else was doing it and, of course, the dominance of discovery-based learning prompted this arrangement. In my mind, I believed this layout would be beneficial to engage the card sorts, carousels, and lots of discovery through talking to their peers. I quickly realised after a few weeks that this layout was not conducive for learning. When I was addressing the class, I would have to ask certain pupils to twist themselves around so they were facing me. On reflection, this was not an effective way of arranging the classroom to support learning for my classroom shape. There are, of course, situations where the arrangements of tables in groups work, for example, in science classrooms. In the context of my classroom layout, the ordering of the tables in groups just didn't work and I reverted to the more traditional layout of rows.

Take a moment to pause and think about your current classroom layout. Draw a quick sketch of your classroom in the box below and include your board(s) and teacher desk positioning.

I suspect it's one of the three layouts: rows, groups of tables or a horseshoe. A study conducted by Gremmen, Van den Berg, Segers and Cillessen (2016) found that 40% of teachers opted for rows, 48% chose to use groups of tables, and 12% decided to use another layout. Thinking back to your own current classroom layout, why did you choose this layout? Have you made changes to your layout over the course of your career? Did something prompt the change? If you did make changes, have you noticed any impact on pupil attention?

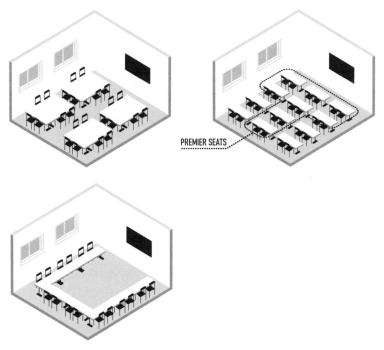

PREMIER SEATS

When considering how we can create the conditions to hit the 'sweet spot' for our explanations and models, one of the first steps is to set up the main arena – your classroom. Cast your mind back to an event you have attended, a meeting, a concert, the cinema. One of the first thoughts as you enter the room is where to sit. Do you sit at the front? Do you hide at the back? This is often dependent upon the event you're attending. We take time to consider our positioning in the room to be in the best spot to ensure we can see and listen to the presenter. We want to feel comfortable. When we feel comfortable and have a good view of the presenter this will contribute towards maintaining our attention. There have been times when I have been late to a meeting or an event and have ended up being situated at the back of the room with a more obscured view. I've often left the meeting or the event less satisfied compared to when I've been able to find my desired seat. Equally, how many times have you been at an event listening to the presenter that has not engaged you? It is harder for us to pay attention to something that doesn't interest us.

How much time do we spend considering the positioning of the seats in our classrooms to ensure all the pupils we teach can listen to our instructions? After all, the attention pupils give to our explanations and models is important to reduce the potential of misconceptions settling in. I remember a few years ago being coached and asked the question about the seating arrangement in my classroom. A particular spot in my classroom meant any pupil sitting at that specific desk would have to arch their neck to track me and listen to my explanation on the board. I never really considered the implication this might have on the pupils sitting at this particular spot in the classroom. If we are seated in a room where we have to arch ourselves in an awkward position it will soon become uncomfortable and our concentration levels will subsequently decrease. Equally, consider a lesson you have recently taught. Reflecting on my own lessons, there have been numerous times when pupils situated further towards the back have been unable to see the board. The dulcet tones of one pupil exclaiming, 'Sir, Charlie's head is in the way and I can't see properly!' It's human nature to 'switch off' when our ability to pay attention is derailed by external factors. To what extent is this impacting our efforts to hit the 'sweet spot'?

A few years ago, I was teaching a Year 7 group that consisted of 32 pupils and, to accommodate them, I had to place a desk at the front of the room next to my whiteboard. It was an unusually large group and there was limited space in the room to fit them in. This was the only place in the room that I could put the desk and, of course, it was a completely different style and colour to the rest of the tables in the classroom. Therefore, it stood out as different to the rest of the tables and chairs in the room. I wonder how much the pupils sitting at this particular desk were able to truly take in my instructions? I wonder just what they were thinking before the lesson? 'Got Mr Chiles next lesson and I don't like sitting at that desk...'

In previous research studies, the role of seating arrangement has not been extensively explored because previous studies have tended to focus on other factors such as lighting, acoustics and room temperature. However, the research that has been conducted on seating arrangements indicates a correlation and, subsequently, demonstrates it can influence learning both positively and negatively. Remember the coach identifying the two pupils who were sitting in that particular spot in my classroom? Research suggests that pupils positioned in what might be deemed a 'poor seating arrangement' could have their learning negatively impacted by 50% (Black, 2007). Decades before Black's findings, other researchers concluded there was a correlation between a student's seating position in the classroom and their academic performance. In more recent studies, Fernandes, Huang and Rinaldo (2011) identified that the layout of a classroom can have an impact on student participation, sense of control, and academic or non-academic activity. Consider for a moment the pupils that are seated at the back of your classroom, irrespective of the seating arrangement. How often do you interact with these pupils?

How often do these pupils actively interact with you? Consider the pupils seated at the side of the classroom.

In 1984, Moore and Glynn discovered a relationship between the number of questions received from a teacher and pupils positioning in the classroom. Pupils seated in a 'more favourable' position in the room were more engaged in questioning and were asked the greatest number of questions by the teacher. The premier seats in the room, whether the layout was rows, horseshoe or groups, were referred to by Marx, Fuhrer and Hartig (2000) as 'T zones' where students in these seats would lead to improved participation and performance compared to those seated elsewhere in the room. Reflecting on my current classroom layout, the premier seats are not where I anticipated they would be. When considering seating plans, one factor that will often influence teachers' decisions on the positioning of pupils is their current performance. For example, pupils who are underperforming are often placed at the front of the classroom so they are more accessible for support. It is possible that these seats may not be the ones where pupils subconsciously receive more attention from the teacher. It could be that the premier seats are positioned elsewhere in your classroom.

Based on Barak Rosenshine's work on the Principles of Instruction (2012), he indicated that the most effective teachers ask lots of questions. When we ask fewer questions or when pupils engage with fewer questions, learning can be impacted negatively. On this basis, could it be possible that pupils seated in the 'premier seats' are inadvertently receiving a greater proportion of the questions asked by the teacher? A further study by Granström (1996) found that pupils situated at the back of the classroom tended to interact more frequently with each other than those seated at the front. This supports the study by Marx, Fuhrer and Hartig (2000). For the pupils situated at the back of the classroom, not in the 'premier seats', their positioning in the room in Granström's study indicated the potential of impacting pupil attention and reducing 'on-task behaviour'.

In comparison, other studies have found that when teachers arrange their seating in a semi-circle (horseshoe shape) there are greater interactions from all pupils. How often do you allow pupils to choose their seating? Consider for a moment, what pupils in your class decide to position themselves at the back of the room? When I think back to my first few years of teaching, the pupils sitting at the back of the class were the ones I needed to speak to the most about 'off-task behaviour'.

Reflecting on these studies when setting up our classroom environment, acknowledging potential 'poor seating' locations and considering strategies to combat these will contribute towards setting up a classroom environment that will be conducive for learning.

Sam's recommendations

1. Consider your classroom layout based on the shape of your room. Does this provide a greater proportion of the premier seats to reduce potential lapses in concentration?
2. Establish a seating layout where possible that alleviates any potential 'poor seating arrangements' and creates more premier seats.
3. Use questioning strategies, such as cold calling so that no matter where pupils are situated in the classroom they know that at some point they may be called upon to contribute to the class discussion.

1.2 The classroom aesthetics

Paying attention is a critical cog to enable learning. After all, we cannot understand, learn or remember that which we do not first attend to. When pupils get distracted, their ability to have a clear understanding of what is being taught diminishes, along with impacting on the learning of others around them. How many times have we become frustrated by the need to repeat instructions multiple times because pupils have not paid attention during the instruction phase? 'Sir, what are we doing again?'

A post by Hobbiss (2017) outlined four main reasons why the role of attention is important.

1. Attention is the gateway to cognition.
2. Attention directly impacts school attainment across the whole spectrum – not just at the lowest end.

3. Attention may mediate other key variables which contribute to school success.
4. Attention skills likely impact our happiness.

In its simplest form, Hobbiss describes attention as the ability to select and process information from the surrounding environment. Prior to the work of Hobbiss, John Ratey (2001) defined attention as being more than just noticing incoming stimuli. He suggested that it involved several processes including filtering out perceptions, balancing multiple perceptions, and attaching emotional significance to these perceptions. Therefore, the greater the number of distractions in the room, the greater the impact these will have on our ability to concentrate.

I'm sure we have all been there in the past. Pupils are listening attentively, or so it would seem until the dreaded wasp enters through the window. Within seconds the attentive class who were listening to your explanation or model, eating out of the palm of your hands, suddenly become distracted, creating a somewhat frenzied environment. Or, the fourth person to visit your classroom looking to speak to one of your pupils. There are many occasions when little events like these throughout the day can have an impact on your pupil's ability to pay attention. They can derail your lesson and lead to fragmentation of knowledge you were wanting pupils to acquire when you spent time planning your lesson. While the event of a wasp entering the classroom is something that is out of your control, if we know aligning attention is important to learning, we can look at other ways to try to minimise any potential distractors in our classrooms.

One of the possible distractors we can minimise and streamline is our use of classroom displays. Just as the layout of the tables was one of the new year considerations, refreshing the classroom displays was of equal importance. I remember spending hours and hours designing new classroom displays during the early stages of my career. On reflection, too many hours were spent creating these displays. At a previous school in the early stages of my career, there was a whole-school competition for departments to create the most interesting classroom displays. As you can imagine, this became quite competitive and beating the history department was of utmost importance. Of course, this approach to encouraging staff to create displays led to some very comprehensive looking displays. The second wave of whole-school updates to these displays came for open evening. Classroom displays are given a high status for influencing prospective parents. I wonder what influence these have on the decisions they made and which school they chose for their child. I would suggest that the conversations parents have with teachers and other parents whose child attends the school probably has greater influence than classroom displays.

When I think back to this focus on classroom displays, the main emphasis was more on how it looked and there was no real focus on the purpose of the display. The purpose of the displays didn't have the role it would play in the learning process at the heart of its design. The time spent cutting out lettering, trying to get the backing sheet flat and deciding on the best border to go with the backing colour. Not to mention the amount of time spent removing old staples from previous displays. This was one of the most frustrating jobs of them all. Hours and hours taking old staples out of the board to replace them with more staples for the new display. On reflection, I'm now convinced that time would have been better spent planning what we were going to teach and how we were going to teach it.

To coincide with the emphasis on discovery-based learning, one year I decided to create a set of interactive displays. I would get pupils to get out of their seats and move their pictures to different places on the display board.

One of the issues with these interactive displays was my desire to get pupils to get out of their seats and actively engage with the information but with limited focus on the knowledge I wanted them to acquire. It was more an opportunity for them to conduct some form of discovery-based learning. My intention was to encourage self-regulation but, ultimately, this wasn't as successful as I had anticipated. I used the displays during one of my performance management observations and it was heralded as outstanding practice but, weeks later, the role it played in the learning process was debatable. Pupils couldn't recall the knowledge we had been looking at from the lesson. The novelty of being able to get out of their seat was the focus rather than having an impact on knowledge retention and supporting learning.

There are other potential reasons why these displays didn't have the intended impact. Firstly, the use of displays such as word walls have their drawbacks because there are just too many keywords in subjects to be able to cover them all on a display. They quickly become outdated and not relevant to the topic being studied. In geography alone, we might be using five or six keywords for a lesson, therefore capturing all of these on a word wall across a whole topic of study wouldn't work. Alongside this, as the topics change throughout the academic year, the display needs to be updated to reflect the change.

In a research study by Fisher, Godwin and Seltman (2014), children were taught six different science lessons with manipulation of the visual classroom environment so that three of the lessons were taught in a heavily decorated classroom while the other three lessons were taught in a sparsely decorated classroom. The study indicated, 'Children were more distracted by the visual environment, spent more time off task, and demonstrated smaller learning gains when the walls were highly decorated than when the decorations were removed.' The study found that for the pupils in the sparsely decorated classroom, the accuracy score on the test questions were higher than those in the decorated classroom. The research also looked at whether pupil attention would defer to another distraction when the visual displays were removed.

Bullard (2010, p. 110) described these distracting visual environments as causing 'visual bombardment' with other researchers, such as Tarr (2004) indicating that over-decorated classroom environments can lead to excessive sensory stimulation. Many of the studies conducted have been in nursery and primary school classrooms with researchers acknowledging that the implication of using extensive visual stimulus on pupil learning in secondary classrooms is not conclusive.

Alongside the potential impact overstimulated classrooms can have on pupils' ability to maintain attention, there is also the consideration of teacher's time. The constant updating of word walls and other displays create an additional workload for teachers, spending hours and hours changing displays to keep them relevant. Is this a practical use of a teacher's time? Inevitably, the first few days of the new academic year allow time to refresh the displays but, all too often, I found they became outdated very quickly and I didn't really have the time to update them. I'm not saying we shouldn't have displays in our classrooms but, given the limited impact they have on learning, time could be better spent focusing on how we plan to deliver our explanations and models. Therefore, streamlining our approach to classroom displays could be a more efficient use of time.

Sam's recommendations

1. Consider the purpose of your displays. Can they be constructed so that they are applicable in the longer term? Consider creating generic subject-based displays that explore how to be an excellent pupil in your subject. These can then be used throughout the academic year and referred to when it is pertinent to do so.
2. Apply a 'less is more' approach to your classroom displays so they don't become an unnecessary distractor.
3. Consider replacing the word walls by filtering and drawing pupils attention to the keywords for the lesson on your whiteboard.
4. Try a clear front wall approach to your classroom design, removing any unnecessary distractions from your teacher stage at the front of the room.

1.3 PowerPoint presentations

Despite all the changes and cycles of pedagogy focus in education from discovery-based learning to direct instruction that teachers have gone through over the last few decades, the PowerPoint presentation has remained a consistent part of every teacher's toolkit. It's a stalwart of the tools teachers have been using to plan their lessons. I'm now in my 14th year of teaching and have not known a time when teachers haven't used PowerPoint as part of their lesson. In many respects, it has become a bit of a safety net when planning and delivering lessons. It is now a common feature of conversations amongst colleagues in departments when determining whether lessons have been planned.

'I've planned the next lesson in the unit. I've put the PowerPoint presentation on the shared drive.'

'Are the PowerPoints ready for our next scheme of work?'
'Have you had a chance to plan the PowerPoints for the next scheme of work?'

There's a danger that the relentless focus on the use of PowerPoints for planning lessons can lead to the PowerPoint becoming 'the lesson'. A 'pretty' PowerPoint presentation doesn't necessarily equate to a well-planned lesson. Similarly, a PowerPoint that is deemed 'boring' doesn't mean the lesson hasn't been well thought out. Irrespective of the state of the PowerPoint presentation, the way the teacher delivers the lesson will be the determining factor to hitting the 'sweet spot' that will contribute towards enabling learning. With this in mind, there should be a shift in the focus in schools to greater thought on the role the teacher plays in the learning process. We will explore this further in the subsequent chapters. For now, we will consider how we can streamline our use of PowerPoints to support – rather than hinder – learning.

All too often, there can be the assumption that a lesson without reliance on a PowerPoint has not been planned. We need to change the status quo and promote the focus on the lesson as being the 'teacher'. The resources we use whilst teaching should be seen as mechanisms to support learning and not deemed the determining factor as to whether a lesson has been planned. This should also be extended to the notion of one branded PowerPoint for all subjects used across the whole school. Recently, I heard of one school insisting on a rigid format to the PowerPoints used by teachers with specific expectations of what should be on each slide. It's somewhat disheartening to hear this because it stifles teacher autonomy to make decisions on how to teach pupils to grasp concepts and processes with the support of a resource like PowerPoint, as and when required. In my experience, enforcing the use of this technology in such a prescribed way doesn't improve the teacher's ability to explain and model but rather hinders it.

In the past, I spent hours in the evening planning my presentations. When I look back at them, they were not effective for several reasons:

1. Too much text on one slide.
2. Font size too small and, therefore, reduces the legibility.
3. Lots of unnecessary transitions and animations.
4. Images that were not sized correctly so became difficult to see.
5. Over the top use of a multitude of fonts and colours.
6. Lack of consistency in the structure of the slides on one PowerPoint file.
7. Too much reliance on reading from the slides.
8. A reluctance to deviate from the intended knowledge and activities outlined on the slides.

Alongside the elaborative designs, the presentations would include the tasks I wanted them to do and there was no wasted space on each slide. I would spend time deciding which transition and animation would work best and generate 'interest' for my pupils. I was very proud of them at the time.

Not only were the presentations very dense and rich in special effects, but I also spent a lot of the time using the PowerPoint to deliver the lesson and not really deviating from the planned activities that I had originally set out to do. However, we know from the research into cognitive science that learning is rather a messy concept and doesn't follow neat chunks that we might expect it to. Therefore, deviating away from the PowerPoint presentation shouldn't be discouraged but rather encouraged. Jones (2003) and Maxwell (2007) support this by indicating that PowerPoint presentations should be used to complement already well-designed lectures and support the learning process.

Cognitive scientists have outlined the complexities of the human mind. It has become a key focus of consideration in education in recent years and its role in supporting learning, The human mind comprises of working and long-term memory and these are primary mechanisms for how we learn (Kirschner, Sweller and Clark, 2006; Winne and Nesbit, 2010). Learning takes place when the information we process in our working memory is transferred and encoded into our long-term memory through a complex network of schema. Therefore, cognitive scientists stress the important role of working memory in processing and encoding information for it to be encoded in our long-term memory.

One of the key challenges for teachers is considering the degree to which our lessons impact pupil's working memory. It is suggested by cognitive scientists that, on average, we can process no more than seven elements at any one time. The implication of our working memory is something we should consider when preparing our lessons. This is something echoed by Kirschner, Sweller and Clark (2006): 'Any instructional theory that ignores the limits of working memory when dealing with novel information or ignores the disappearance of those limits when dealing with familiar information is unlikely to be effective.' It is very easy for teachers to overburden a pupil's working memory and cause cognitive overload, especially when we are teaching new knowledge. When our PowerPoints are dense with lots of information, colours and transitions this can be cognitively distracting. This is further impacted when we read from information from the PowerPoint as well as displaying it at the time.

Numerous research studies have been conducted to assess the role of using PowerPoint in education to enhance learning. Many of these studies have been based on the impact they have at university level. In one of the studies conducted, it was concluded that PowerPoint has 'no measurable influence on course performance and minimal effect on grades' (Hill et al, 2012).

In contrast, in the studies exploring the influence of PowerPoint on learning, students rated their lessons higher and preferred it when teachers used PowerPoints in their lectures (Drouin et al, 2013). This was further supported by a study conducted on English lessons in secondary schools which found that pupils supported the use of PowerPoint presentations with 67% of pupils strongly agreeing that the lessons with PowerPoint were more interesting.

In recent years, I have invested less time in preparing the look of these presentations and more importance on the content and how this content is presented. Not only have I streamlined the presentations I use in lessons I have also not used PowerPoints for any part of a lesson. There are times when your expertise of the subject, storytelling with hand-drawn sketches and passion for what you are teaching is all that is needed to deliver the knowledge that you want your pupils to know. After all, as we have already said in this section, you are ultimately the lesson and sharing your knowledge of the subject through a means other than a PowerPoint presentation should be encouraged and not discouraged through rigid school policies. The example below resembles the presentations that I use for lessons today.

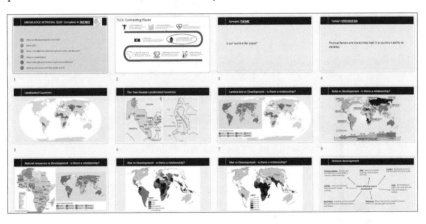

In an article by Andy Tharby (2019), he outlined some key ways we can use PowerPoints more effectively to reduce cognitive overload. In the following graphic, I have summarised some of the key points Andy highlighted along with others that I would recommend.

1. Reduce the amount of content on each slide. Aim for one photo/diagram that is clear. Keep text to a minimum.	2. Integrate labels with diagrams so that pupils can look at the text and images simultaneously.	3. Remove any unnecessary images that are not related to what you want pupils to learn.	4. Avoid the use of 'over the top' transitions to make the PowerPoint seem 'interesting'. These will act as a distractor.
5. Consider the colour scheme and keep this consistent across one presentation.	6 Use arrows to illustrate connections between images.	7. Use icons to indicate what you are expecting pupils to do when presenting specific slides.	8. If you are expecting pupils to use images, provide a handout and allow them access to the presentation for future reference.
9. Avoid reading text aloud that is on the slide. When explaining, blank the presentation to make you the focal point.	10. Remove unnecessary backgrounds when sharing key vocabulary.	11. When sharing key points, do this one at a time, giving pupils space between each new idea presented.	12. Aim to explain images/diagrams rather than having extended text underneath or at the side.

Sam's recommendations

1. Reflect on your current PowerPoint presentations. Are they creating cognitive overload?
2. Remember you are the lesson and not the PowerPoint. Embrace opportunities to teach without the reliance on the use of a pre-prepared presentation.

1.4 Classroom resources

It's Monday morning and you've had a hectic start to the day getting the family ready and rushing to drop the children off at nursery. You get into work and remember you didn't photocopy that resource you needed for period 1. Not to worry, you check the time, and you will just be able to get it sorted before the lesson starts. However, you arrive at the photocopier to find the standard morning frantic queue of colleagues getting prepared for the day.

I'm sure this scenario is an all too familiar one that most teachers have found themselves in at some point in their careers. It can often feel like the wind is taken right from underneath our feet as the panic sets in on what we will do without the resource. It can unsettle what seemed like a well-planned lesson. I do wonder about the number of hours teachers have spent stood at the photocopying machine waiting for class sets of resources to finish printing. There's always that one colleague who decides to leave all their printing to do in one go and the comment, *'I've got quite a bit to do'* can leave you feeling frustrated. The hours spent at photocopiers is only one small part of the potential issues we find ourselves in with classroom resources. The money schools give over to photocopying costs and the continual maintenance of the machines that break down on a regular basis questions the true value we get out of the hours it takes to provide pupils with the resources. This is coupled with the time invested in creating resources for lessons that may just be acting as a tool to suggest pupils are completing work, a poor proxy for learning.

Mary Myatt in her book *Back on Track* indicates some of the issues with our obsession with photocopying: 'Why does so much photocopying go on in schools? One response might be that it saves time, to which a further question might be, it saves time to do what? Another response might be that we need the sheets as resources to use in class. Again, it is reasonable to ask why. It's as if producing photocopied resources has become a crutch, as if a lesson can't happen unless we have a pile of papers under our arms to present to a class.'

Much like the reliance on the use of PowerPoints, in education the use of resources has become a similar safety blanket to delivering a lesson or for it to be perceived that a lesson has been planned because pupils have resources in front of them. Worksheets can be a useful tool to support learning but this depends on the intention and design of the worksheet used. Research studies have demonstrated that well-designed worksheets have a positive impact on pupils' learning (Sasmaz-Oren and Ormanci, 2012). However, poorly designed worksheets can equally hinder learning (Lesley and Labbo, 2003).

In the past, I have been guilty of designing worksheets with the intention of it being a teaching tool rather than a learning tool. A typical worksheet I designed would include an extract of a newspaper article or a section from a textbook. I would then include a series of questions that I wanted pupils to answer. The main issue was that I expected pupils to 'discover' the answers from the source of text provided, with minimal input from me before the task. Essentially, the worksheets I created were there for my pupils to work independently.

Retrospectively, using worksheets in this way is counterproductive in the pursuit of learning. Adopting this approach would inevitably result in my pupils struggling with the questions, they would leave them out, or require support from me in order to put pen to paper. Of course, there were always some pupils who were able to answer the questions but it didn't encourage deeper level thinking. From my experience and the research studies conducted, worksheets are more effective when they are designed to act as a learning tool to consolidate and reflect on knowledge that has been explained and modelled by you as the teacher.

Based on this, a more effective approach to incorporating worksheets into our lessons is when our pupils are novices and learning new information, after first explaining and modelling. This is emphasised by John Sweller (2021) in his most recent paper: 'The worked example effect clearly indicates the importance of explicit instruction when learners are presented with novel information. Problem solving only becomes viable as a learning procedure once learners are sufficiently expert to require practice of a specific procedure. It does not work as an introduction to a new topic as confirmed by the many studies of the expertise reversal effect.'

Once pupils have developed their schema for the content being taught we can then use worksheets to provide time for reviewing and reflecting. I wish I had used this approach in the early stages of my career but, at this time, pedagogy in my school was focused on teacher's being facilitators of learning and pupils were left to discover with minimal guidance.

Chapter summary

- Seating arrangements and its role in learning indicates a correlation, it can influence learning both positively and negatively.
- When pupils are seated in a 'more favourable' position in the room it can lead to greater engagement in answering questions as well as being asked questions by the teacher.
- When there are increasing distractions during a lesson this will impede pupils ability to concentrate.
- Apply a 'less is more' approach to the use of classroom resources so that time can be invested in crafting and practising our explanations and models.

- Classroom resources should be seen as mechanisms to support learning and not deemed the determining factor as to whether a lesson has been planned.
- PowerPoints that are dense with lots of information, colours and transitions can be cognitively distracting and counterintuitive to supporting learning.
- Worksheets are more effective when they are designed to act as a learning tool rather than a teaching tool.

Chapter resources

To support the discussion of how we can streamline our classrooms to make them efficient and effective to enable learning, a visual summary that captures the key points in this first chapter can be found via the QR code below. You may find this helpful when revisiting some of the research and theories in your own department or school. These could be used as a tool to review and reflect when considering how to streamline your classroom(s).

HTTPS://BIT.LY/SWEETSPOTCS01

References

Black, S. (2007) 'Achievement by design', *American School Board Journal*, 194(10), 39-41.

Bullard, J. (2010) *Creating environments for learning: Birth to age eight.* Upper Saddle River, NJ: Prentice Hall.

Drouin, M., Hile, R. E., Vartanian, L. R. and Webb, J. (2013) 'Student Preferences for Online Lecture Formats', *Quarterly Review of Distance Education*, 14(3), 151-162.

Fernandes, A. C., Huang, J. and Rinaldo, V. J. (2011) 'Does Where a Student Sits Really Matter? The Impact of Seating Locations on Student Classroom Learning', *International Journal of Applied Educational Studies*, 10(1).

Fisher, A., Godwin, K. and Seltman, H. (2014) 'Visual Environment, Attention Allocation, and Learning in Young Children: When Too Much of a Good Thing May Be Bad', *Psychological Science*, 25(7).

Granström, K. (1996) 'Private Communication Between Students in the Classroom in Relation to Different Classroom Features', *Educational Psychology*, 16(4), 349-364.

Gremmen, M. C., van den Berg, Y. H. M., Segers, E. and Cillessen, A. H. N. (2016) 'Considerations for classroom seating arrangements and the role of teacher characteristics and beliefs', *Social Psychology of Education: An International Journal*, 19(4), 749-774.

Hill, A., Arford, T., Lubitow, A. and Smollin, L. (2012) 'I'm Ambivalent about It: The Dilemmas of PowerPoint', *Teaching Sociology*, 40(3), 242-256.

Hobbiss, M. (2017) 'Pay attention! Why I think it is important to study attention in school children', *The Hobblog* [Blog] 7 October. Retrieved from: www.bit.ly/3inHJee

Jones, A. M. (2003) 'The use and abuse of PowerPoint in Teaching and Learning in the Life Sciences: A Personal Overview', *Bioscience Education*, 2(1), 1-13.

Kirschner, P. A., Sweller, J. and Clark, R. E. (2006) 'Why Minimal Guidance During Instruction Does Not Work: An Analysis of the Failure of Constructivist, Discovery, Problem-Based, Experiential, and Inquiry-Based Teaching', *Educational Psychologist*, 41(2), 75-86.

Lesley, M. and Labbo, L. D. (2003) 'A pedagogy of control: Worksheets and the special need child', *Language Arts*, 80(6), 444.

Marx, A., Fuhrer, U. and Hartig, T. (2012) 'Effects of Classroom Seating Arrangements on Children's question-asking', *Learning Environments Research*, 2, 249-263.

Maxwell, A. (2007) 'Ban the Bullet-Point! – Content-Based PowerPoint for Historians', *The History Teacher*, 4(1), 39-54.

Myatt, M. (2020) *Back on Track.* Woodbridge: John Catt Educational.

Ratey, J. (2001) *A User's Guide to the Brain: Perception, Attention, and the Four Theaters of the Brain.* New York, NY: Vintage.

Rosenshine, B. (2012) 'Principles of Instruction: Research-Based Strategies That All Teachers Should Know', *American Educator*, Spring, 12-39.

Sasmaz-Oren, F. & Ormanci, U. (2012) 'An application about pre-service teachers' development and use of worksheets and an evaluation of their opinions about the application', *Educational Sciences: Theory and Practice*, 12 (1), 263–270.

Sweller, J. (2021) 'Why Inquiry-based Approaches Harm Students' Learning'. Sydney: The Centre for Independent Studies.

Tarr, P. (2004) 'Consider the Walls', *Beyond the Journal.* May. Retrieved from: www.bit.ly/2TC1fvh

Winne, P. H. and Nesbit, J. C. (2010) *The Psychology of Academic Achievement.* Retrieved from: www.bit.ly/3rChVPy

2

PREPARING YOUR PITCH

'Those who can, do. Those who understand teach.'
– Lee S. Schulman

2.1 Knowing thy subject

It probably seems obvious that teachers need to have good subject knowledge in order to support pupils to learn and perform well throughout their education journey. Ball (1991) indicated, 'Teachers cannot help children learn things they themselves do not understand.' When we apply for a new teaching post, one of the essential aspects of the person specification is strong subject knowledge. This is because evidence suggests there is a strong connection between teacher subject knowledge and pupil performance. Creating a positive relationship between subject knowledge and pupil performance has more to it than we might first believe. Passing knowledge on to pupils that enables them to become successful geographers, historians, writers, mathematicians and so on involves more than just knowing our subject but having a strong subject knowledge base is the first step to success.

In the most recent Pisa tests conducted by OECD, some of the top-performing education systems are Singapore and Finland. The Programme for International Student Assessment creates an education ranking for countries based on international tests completed in maths, reading and science by 15-year-old pupils. The tests are conducted every three years creating a global school league table. Since its introduction, UK schools have remained mid-table performers whilst Singapore has remained one of the highest-performing education systems. So, why has Singapore continued to have one of the best performing education systems in the world? Since it became an independent country in 1965, the government has focused on developing its economy through improving education with the country recruiting its teachers from the top 5% of graduates in the system. The vice-president of Nanyang Technology University, Professor Sing Kong Lee, previously commented on the reason for Singapore's success, 'Singapore invested heavily in a quality teaching force – to raise up the prestige and status of teaching and to attract the best graduates.'

This connection was emphasised by Machin and Murphy (2011) who concluded that 'having a very effective, rather than average teacher raises each pupil's attainment by a third of a grade'. However, during the early stages of my career, there wasn't really a tremendous focus on the importance of subject knowledge but rather on the ability of teachers to develop pupil's ability to build transferable skills. Setting up discovery-based learning and building PLC skills was a key priority in the education sector during this time. It was perceived as a given that trainee teachers would have secure subject knowledge, after all they have just completed a degree in the subject. But there is a difference between knowing your subject and knowing how to teach it to pupils. When we consider the factors that lead to effective pedagogy, there are three key aspects to explore in relation to how teachers behave:

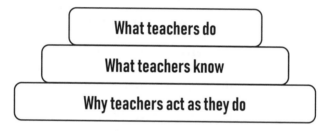

How many times have you glanced over a PowerPoint the same day as you're about to teach a lesson that a colleague has planned in your department? Inevitably, when you attempt to deliver the lesson, it doesn't always go to plan because you haven't been involved in the intricacy of the planning stage. How one teacher approaches teaching the subject will have subtle differences depending upon previous experience of teaching the concept and expertise in that specific aspect of the subject. When we attempt to deliver a lesson that we are insecure about, this can create challenges because it can derail the control we have in the clarity of our explanations.

Teaching is complex and many researchers have recognised the challenges teachers face, acknowledging this is attributed to the different types of knowledge used during the teaching and learning process. Shulman (1987) suggested that teachers need to have seven knowledge bases in order to effectively teach. These knowledge bases are:

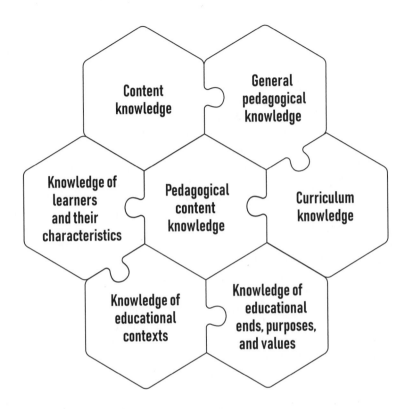

This was further emphasised by an extensive report from The Sutton Trust (Coe, Aloisi, Higgins and Major, 2014) reviewing the evidence for 'What makes great teaching?'. One of these components was pedagogical content knowledge: 'The most effective teachers have deep knowledge of the subjects they teach, and when teachers' knowledge falls below a certain level it is a significant impediment to students' learning. As well as a strong understanding of the material being taught, teachers must also understand the ways students think about the content, be able to evaluate the thinking behind students' own methods, and identify students' common misconceptions.'

The concept of pedagogical content knowledge was defined by Shulman (1986) as: 'Embodies the aspects of content most germane to its teachability. Within the category of pedagogical content knowledge I include, for the most regularly taught topics in one's subject area, the most useful forms of representation of those ideas, the most powerful analogies, illustrations, examples, explanations, and demonstrations – in a word, the ways of representing and formulating the subject that make it comprehensible to others... [It] also includes an understanding of what makes the learning of specific concepts easy or difficult: the conceptions and preconceptions that students of different ages and backgrounds bring with them to the learning.'

From Shulman's definition of pedagogical content knowledge, it can be considered something that is unique to teachers – combining teachers' pedagogical knowledge (how to teach) and subject knowledge (understanding what we are teaching). Therefore, being knowledgeable in your subject discipline is only the first step in truly knowing thy subject. To enable effective teaching and learning that provides the springboard for setting up your explanations and models, this knowledge should be developed alongside an understanding of how to teach your subject. For example, this is what defines science teachers from scientists and history teachers from historians. This is because teachers will organise and deliver their subject knowledge in a different way to best support the pupils being taught. In comparison, scientists and historians will use their knowledge to undertake research and use that research to inform new discoveries or developments within their field of expertise. Hauslein et al (1992) found that science teachers demonstrated a more rigid structure to their knowledge in comparison to researchers, which he believed was attributed to the constraints teachers are placed under from curriculum demands.

In a study conducted by Hashweh (1987), three physics teachers and three biology teachers were asked to evaluate a textbook chapter and then plan a unit of study based on the material from the chapter. One of the concepts the biology teachers were asked to plan was photosynthesis and evidence from the research indicated that these teachers were already aware of the potential misconceptions pupils may have. Equally, the teachers knew what the pupils might find most difficult to understand and considered these when planning. When the biology teachers were asked to consider the physics concepts, they could only demonstrate general ideas about how to teach the concepts, which was different to their in-depth awareness of the biology concepts. This was a similar outcome for the physics teachers when asked to consider the biology concepts. Hashweh (1987) indicated the importance of a teacher's subject knowledge, demonstrating that when teachers were asked about subject concepts, not based on their field of expertise, they demonstrated more misconceptions, lack of understanding and struggled to organise the information when preparing how to deliver the concepts for teaching to a class.

The importance of subject knowledge was reinforced by an extensive review from the Evidence Based Education (2020), which indicates the role of teacher's subject knowledge as one of the core dimensions to great teaching. 'Great teachers understand the content they are teaching and how it is learnt.

This means teachers should have deep and fluent knowledge and a flexible understanding of the content they are teaching and how it is learnt, including its inherent dependences. They should have an explicit repertoire of well-crated explanations, examples and tasks for each topic they teach.'

This extensive study, along with Hashweh's, demonstrates the importance of knowing the intricacies of your subject to be able to modify resources to present material to pupils in a meaningful way that ultimately supports learning. This level of pedagogical content knowledge comes from experience and taking the time to reflect on the concepts in your subject. In the early stages of my career, I was developing my pedagogical content knowledge as I taught different aspects of the subject that I may not have necessarily done in-depth at university. It is important that, as teachers, we recognise this level of knowledge will take time to develop and knowing the intricacies of our subject is something that we build over time. We will explore this further later on in this chapter.

Sam's recommendations

1. Strong subject knowledge is one of the core pillars to preparing lessons.
2. Pedagogical content knowledge is distinctive to teachers that encapsulates the understanding of subject concepts and how to teach them.
3. Having strong subject knowledge is the first step to finding 'the sweet spot' to delivering precise explanations and models.
4. A fluent and flexible understanding of the subject concepts taught is something that teachers develop over time with practice.

2.2 Knowledge 360

In its simplest form, the skill of teaching is about transforming the knowledge that is to be taught in a way that is effectively processed, understood, strengthens pupil schema and, subsequently, used independently in new contexts over time.

So, if knowledge is a key factor in preparing a teacher's pitch for delivering expert explanations and models, there is a side to knowledge that can provide

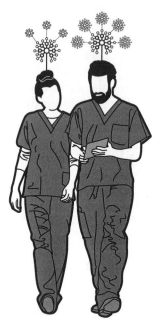

an obstacle to navigate mastery execution. This obstacle to be mindful of when preparing the pitch is the curse of knowledge, which is often referred to as a cognitive or egocentric bias. The curse of knowledge can strike when an expert in their field doesn't take into account other people's knowledge base. The phrase first appeared on the scene in a paper written by economists Camerer, Loewenstein and Weber (1989). The aim of their research was to investigate whether those with more knowledge would be able to predict the judgements of those with less knowledge.

Take the example of an experienced doctor communicating with training junior doctors. When the experienced doctor delivers their training, they may not take into account prior understanding of their students, leading to them struggling to communicate their expertise. Equally, think back to a time when you have assumed that someone understands what you are talking about and the surprise you have shown when they don't and you have to explain it to them. It is something that we do without a second thought because we assume that people will have similar knowledge to us.

One example of a study to illustrate the curse of knowledge was published by Newton (1990), known as the 'tapping study'. Participants were randomly assigned as a tapper or a listener. Tappers were tasked with finger tapping on a desk three tunes which they selected from a list of 25 popular songs. Following this, they were asked to make a decision on whether the listeners would be able to successfully identify the songs that they had been tapping. Overall, the tappers suggested that the listeners would on average be able to identify the song based on their finger tapping. However, the listeners were not as successful at identifying the songs as expected by the listeners. The tapping study indicated how the curse of knowledge can affect people's judgement. The tappers assumed that because they knew the song they were tapping, the listeners would also know the song.

For school teachers, being mindful of the curse of knowledge is a factor we might consider when preparing our lessons. Teachers spend many hours planning lessons with the ultimate aim to create experiences that enable pupils to become more knowledgeable in the subjects they are studying. The extent of a teacher's knowledge is something that has been built up over time through practice. We have, in effect, become unconsciously competent in our subject knowledge having developed extensive schema over time. This can pose difficulties when it comes to planning and delivering lessons. Therefore, we shouldn't assume that pupils know something just because we do.

The more we teach our curriculum, the more we develop and deepen our knowledge to create greater automaticity in knowledge recall. There have been many occasions in recent years when pupils have asked how I can just recall key facts and figures related to historical tropical storm events such as Typhoon Haiyan. I find this is a great opportunity to share the science of learning with pupils and talk about the role of continually bringing knowledge back to mind to strengthen future recall. I remind the pupils I teach that it isn't about teachers having special powers that enables them to recall knowledge easily as they perceive it but more the process of continually reviewing and recalling knowledge over time.

When planning lessons, having an awareness of pupils' prior knowledge is important to create lessons that build on that knowledge. We identified at the beginning of the chapter that just having subject knowledge isn't the magic bullet to supporting pupils to learn. The role of the teacher is to take the extensive knowledge we have of our subject and present it in a way that our pupils will understand and can subsequently develop their own schemas. We will explore this further in chapter 3 as we look at how we deliver our pitch by turning the abstract concepts into concrete examples that pupils will understand. For now, we will continue our focus on preparing the pitch.

The following diagram, designed by Efrat Furst, provides a visual explanation of constructing a knowledge base.

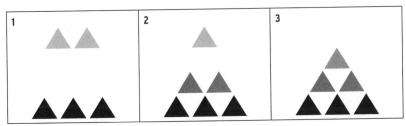

Furst describes the construction of knowledge through the analogy of building a pyramid with each new piece of knowledge, represented by the lighter grey triangle, placed on top of existing knowledge, the dark grey triangles. The correct alignment of existing knowledge to new knowledge is consolidated and processed to move from surface to deep level thinking. Furst indicates when pupils are encouraged to consolidate new information into networks of existing information (already established schemas containing prior knowledge) we should be mindful of the following three components:

- The new concept.
- The existing knowledge to be associated with the new concept.
- Meaningful association between them.

For new connections to form and knowledge to build, the three components should be active when pupils are learning. The extent to which new and existing knowledge is consolidated and meaningful connections made will affect future understanding. With all of this in mind, having a clear understanding of the knowledge to be taught and how it builds together to form the curriculum is an important element in preparing a teacher's pitch. This is where building curriculums collaboratively as a department can help to support the effective designing of lesson experiences for pupils. If our explanations and models are to be effective and connected to the fundamental concepts and processes that make up our subject, teachers need to be involved in the designing and continued reviewing of the curriculum. It should be something that should be 'done with' rather than 'done to' teachers.

It should not be seen as the teacher's role to merely 'deliver' the curriculum that has been created by the subject lead. This process of top-down delivery of curriculums 'on a plate' can be done with all the best intentions to reduce teacher workload. However, it will inevitably lead to a disconnect between the intention of the curriculum, teacher delivery and pupils' experiences. This, in turn, will consequently lead to increased teacher workload and anxiety when planning lessons, having the opposite effect of what was originally intended through the weighting of curriculum design falling on subject leads.

When teachers are not involved in the mechanics of curriculum development, leaders can unintentionally deskill teachers and reduce teacher morale. Equally, teachers given free rein to create a scheme of work can be just as counterintuitive. I remember, in the first few years of my career, being handed a topic of study and asked to plan a scheme of work based on that topic. This was accompanied by the suggestion of a textbook to use to create this scheme. The objective was to plan a scheme of work on tectonics. At this point in my career, designing a coherent scheme of work that considered previously taught knowledge, misconceptions and prior knowledge wasn't something I considered when planning the unit. A combination of being a novice at planning a scheme of work and the lack of guidance during my training were factors that undermined my ability to plan a coherent scheme. I needed some guidance and an opportunity to collaborate with planning the series of lessons. At that stage in my career, I was given too much autonomy. There needs to be a balance in the collaboration of curriculum development.

In a report from the National Foundation for Education Research (Worth and Van den Brande, 2020), one of the key findings was a positive relationship between teacher autonomy and higher job satisfaction. Alongside this finding there was an identification that while teachers tend to have greater autonomy over planning individual lessons, this isn't always the case when it comes to contributing towards planning the curriculum and associated assessments: 'Teachers report relatively high autonomy over classroom activities, including the teaching methods they use and how they plan and prepare lessons, but lower autonomy over curriculum, assessment and their professional development goals.'

If we want teachers to deliver expert explanations and share their passion for the subject we need them to be involved in the process. How can we do this? We need to find the balance between effective collaboration and intelligent autonomy steered by subject leaders. The following are several suggestions that subject leaders and teachers could do when preparing their pitch:

- Create curriculum partners within departments where newly qualified teachers work with more experienced teachers to guide them through the curriculum and lesson planning.
- Use department time to work collaboratively in reviewing and planning changes to the curriculum. Provide opportunities for more experienced teachers to share their experiences of teaching difficult concepts and processes, along with the rationale for the curriculum sequencing.
- For newly qualified teachers, find time to regularly ask questions, share ideas, and discuss how to prepare your pitch.
- When reviewing previously taught units of study, reflect on the misconceptions that pupils had and build in time to discuss how to reduce these misconceptions. For example, this might involve looking at alternative resources to the ones that were used by teachers or considering whether the order of teaching the concepts might need changing to support pupils achieving mastery.

In schools, there is often a disproportionate focus on 'how' the subject is taught through developing pedagogy over subject expertise. The drive to become research-informed can lead teachers down a rabbit hole of trying to implement the next edu-fad in their classroom, whilst neglecting the main thing which is an understanding of the intricacies of the subject we are teaching because, ultimately, we can have a range of different ways to teach our subject but without the underpinning knowledge to do so this will impact the quality of our explanations and models. The power of pedagogy is determined by the power of the teacher's knowledge of what they are teaching and why they are teaching it in a particular sequence.

Now that we have invested time in developing our understanding of the rationale for curriculum sequencing it is then the planning and preparing the individual lessons for the pupils we have been assigned to teach. This is where we spend time personalising our lessons.

Sam's recommendations

1. The curse of knowledge is a cognitive bias that occurs when experts fail to take into account others may not know what they do.
2. Navigating the curse of knowledge is a factor to consider when planning lessons to avoid assumptions about pupils' understanding of our subject.
3. Considering pupils' prior knowledge during the planning phase is crucial to preparing a successful pitch.
4. The way new and existing knowledge is processed and consolidated can affect future understanding.
5. Teachers should have knowledge of the requirements of their subject curriculum and how it is sequenced to build in complexity over time.

2.3 Upgrading the curriculum

Mary Myatt has talked passionately about curriculum making and the need to deliver lessons for pupils that are 'above their pay grade' (2020). We owe it to our pupils to 'pitch up' our lessons and create rigorous and challenging lessons that put pupils in what Andy Tharby and Shaun Allison (2015) referred to as the 'struggle zone'. During the first few years of my career, there was a big focus on the concept of the gifted and talented pupils, with some schools having a specific role for a member staff to be the gifted and talented coordinator. This was the case in the first school I taught at where there was a designated member of staff who planned and implemented strategies with teachers across the school, raising awareness of which pupils in our school were gifted and talented. This extended with the whole school gifted and talented register where teachers were directed to signpost their gifted and talented pupils on their lesson plans. Departments were also asked to nominate a gifted and talented representative for each subject and these teachers would meet to discuss the strategies for stretching and challenging this group of pupils. While the school identified pupils they believed were gifted and talented, departments were also required to name pupils they considered gifted and talented, along with the strategies being used in lessons to support these pupils.

On reflection, this was possibly one of the reasons why, for many years, schools went down the route of differentiated outcomes, using bronze, silver and gold descriptors, as well as the multitude of resources and designated tasks created by teachers for specific groups of pupils in lessons. The problem is that we inevitably created a glass ceiling for what pupils could achieve in our lessons. We sent out a message that not all of our pupils could achieve the highest outcomes or that a select few were expected to achieve the highest outcomes through the labels we placed over their heads. At the same time, we gave pupils the option to not challenge themselves and that doing the bare minimum – the bronze outcome – the 'all must' objective was somehow acceptable. We set pupils up to potentially fail regardless of the label we applied, which leads to increased anxiety in both teachers and pupils.

When we plan lessons that look to challenge *all* of our pupils and 'pitch up' our explanations, we create a culture of high aspirations. We want all pupils to believe that, when we are learning something, we should expect it to be challenging and take us into the struggle zone. If we go for the easy option then we end up with surface-level thinking, low aspirations and low attainment. When we pitch up our lessons for all pupils, aspirations rise and everyone feels like they can achieve no matter what. This is a culture of high aspirations and a belief that a healthy struggle is necessary for learning.

The Pygmalion effect is an example of how high expectations can lead to better performance. The term originates back to the story of Pygmalion, a mythical Greek sculptor. In the story, Pygmalion carved a statue of a woman and then became obsessed with it. He appealed to Aphrodite, the goddess of love, to bring the statue to life because he was unable to love a human. The goddess took pity on him and brought the statue to life.

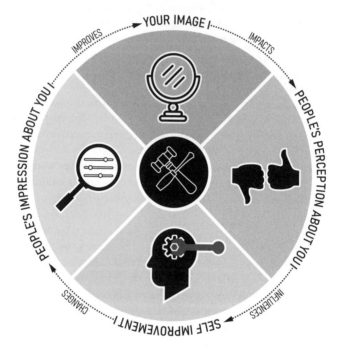

This was illustrated in a study conducted by Robert Rosenthal and Lenore Jacobson (1968) who examined the influence of teacher expectations on pupil performance. Their research involved testing the IQ of elementary school pupils. Their teachers were told that the IQ test indicated that approximately one-fifth of their pupils had above average intelligence. The 'gifted' pupils were chosen at random so that they did not have any significant statistical advantage over their peers. After the study had finished, all pupils had their IQs retested with both groups of pupils showing an improvement. However, the pupils who were described as 'gifted' experienced greater gains in their IQ scores. Rosenthal and Jacobson believed that these results from the study could be attributed to the Pygmalion effect, where teachers paid more attention to the 'gifted' pupils, offering them more support and encouragement.

Take a moment to think about your teaching timetable and the different groups you have been assigned to teach. Is there a particular group that you dread teaching each week? Or, is there a specific group that you see as not having the same potential as another that are in the same year? Consider how you perceive these teaching groups and how you portray your thoughts of the groups you teach to other colleagues.

Historical views about teaching groups, especially when they are 'set' can inevitably lead to teachers having low expectations and, therefore, create a low aspiration culture amongst specific groups. Not only does it create low expectations with teachers, when groups are set according to their ability it can result in pupils knowing they are in a lower set and generating a self-fulfilling prophecy of low aspirations. If we are to raise the expectations from teachers and, in turn, raise the overall aspirations of our pupils, we need to take away the 'labels' and have a mindset that *all* pupils can achieve. John F. Kennedy once said in a speech, 'The rising tide lifts all the boats.' When there is a culture of high expectations from staff regardless of the teaching group, it can contribute towards raising the aspirations of all pupils. We need to build in and encourage resilience when faced with challenging work and not shy away from this by creating lessons that lack challenge.

All too often, as teachers, we can get bogged down in the delivery of lessons to match the ultimate destination pit stops of GCSE and A Level exams.

GP Guided Practice
IP Independent Practice
⭐ Success

This leads to some school leaders and teachers believing that raising aspirations for pupils is about bringing GCSE style questions into KS3 and similarly bringing A Level language into GCSE. While this might raise aspirations, our core purpose as teachers is not about supporting pupils to become great at passing an OCR Maths exam or an Edexcel Geography exam. If this is our core purpose as teachers, we have lost sight of what our role is. You might say, but this is how we are measured as teachers! After all, in many schools, our credibility is based upon these results.

While this might be the case, I would argue that focusing on this when planning our lessons provides a tunnelled vision on the notion of success. Teaching isn't about supporting pupils to navigate exam specification, it is about guiding and supporting pupils to develop mastery knowledge and skills for each of the subjects they study. We want them to be excellent mathematicians, historians, geographers and athletes. We want them to be able to apply this knowledge to different contexts and use it as a lever to the next stage of their education journey. If we do this the performance indicators (for example, GCSE exams) will demonstrate this as pupils will have mastered the knowledge and skills.

Sam's recommendations

1. When planning lessons we should aim to pitch them up to create rigour and challenge that activates deep level thinking.
2. We should create a culture in our classrooms that promotes high aspirations.
3. Our historical views about teaching groups can result in teachers having low expectations and therefore create a low aspiration culture amongst specific groups.
4. We need to build pupil resilience to tackling challenging work and build this in to prepare our lesson pitch.
5. Our role as teachers isn't based on exam specifications but rather about creating lessons that layer knowledge to support pupils to master the subjects they are studying.

2.4 Enhancing subject knowledge

When I taught at Culcheth High School, one of the key messages for teachers was the hashtag #alwayslearning. This hashtag was regularly used to share the vision that no matter what stage of your teaching career, we are always learning new ways to teach our subject. This message was regularly revisited and built into the CPD curriculum. Equally, this can be applied to our subject knowledge. This was echoed by Dylan Wiliam (2019) who said, 'If we create a culture where every teacher believes they need to improve, not because they are not good enough but because they can be even better, there is no limit to what we can achieve.'

As outlined in the Great Teaching Toolkit (Coe, Rauch, Kime, Singleton and Education Endowment Foundation, 2020), teachers should have a wide repertoire of examples to turn abstract concepts in our subjects to develop pupils' understanding. We have outlined in this chapter the role of subject knowledge as one of the key ingredients to successful teaching. For example, when I'm teaching pupils to understand the impact of deforestation, I need to be able to draw on my wider knowledge of climate change, soil functionality, and the implications of the hydrological cycle. Alongside having knowledge of these interrelated concepts, I also need to be able to draw on concrete examples. This will require me to have kept up-to-date with my subject knowledge and continually review it.

There are a number of ways we can work to continually develop our subject knowledge:

- Use resources published by subject associations to keep up with developments in your subject. An example of an association for my subject is The Geographical Association. They provide a wealth of literature to support the continued improvement of teacher knowledge. The association will often publish articles on how teachers have approached difficult concepts in their own classrooms as well as an enhancement for specific concepts that have changed as a result of new research.
- Join in with conversations on social media platforms, such as Twitter, where teachers share how they approach the teaching of difficult concepts and share articles to signpost examples of key pieces of research to update subject concepts.
- Learn from the expertise of other colleagues in your departments; ask them to provide workshops to enhance the knowledge of others. For example, geography colleagues will have expertise in either physical or human geography and may have focused on niche concepts that they can share to upskill the rest of the department. In English, a colleague

may have focused on one specific novel that the school teaches to pupils. The additional expertise of this teacher could be used to support other colleagues.

Ultimately, if we create opportunities for teachers to develop both their knowledge of the subject they teach, along with the most effective pedagogy approaches, this will provide the foundations for preparing our pitch to have the biggest impact on learning.

Chapter summary

- Research suggests there is a strong connection between teacher subject knowledge and pupil performance.
- There are three key aspects to consider in relation to how teachers behave: what teachers do, what teachers know, why teachers act as they do.
- When we deliver a lesson that we are insecure about, this can affect the clarity of our explanations.
- Knowing your subject is the first step to effective teaching and learning and this knowledge should be developed alongside an understanding of how to teach your subject.
- Being aware of the intricacies of your subject is important to be able to present material to pupils in a meaningful way that ultimately supports learning.
- Being mindful of the curse of knowledge is a factor we might consider when preparing our lessons.
- Having a clear understanding of the knowledge to be taught and how it builds together to form the curriculum is an important element in preparing a teacher's pitch.
- Building curriculums collaboratively as a department can help to support the effective design of lesson experiences for pupils.
- When we plan lessons that look to challenge all of our pupils and 'pitch up' our explanations, we create a culture of high aspirations.

Chapter resources

Similar to the first chapter, the QR code below provides a summary poster to support teachers and leaders in preparing their pitch to make them efficient and effective to enable learning. The summary captures the key points shared in this second chapter. In the next chapter, we will unpick the delivery of our explanations and models to hit the sweet spot.

HTTPS://BIT.LY/SWEETSPOTCS02

References

Ball, D. L. (1991) 'Research on teaching mathematics: Making subject matter knowledge part of the equation'. In J. Brophy (Ed.), *Advances in research on teaching*, 2, 1-47. Greenwich, CT: JAI.

Camerer, C. F., Loewenstein, G. and Weber, M. (1989) 'The Curse of Knowledge in Economic Settings: An Experimental Analysis', *Journal of Political Economy*, 97(5), 1232-1254.

Coe, R., Aloisi, C., Higgins, S. and Major, L. E. (2014) What makes great teaching? *Review of the underpinning research*. London: The Sutton Trust. Retrieved from: www.bit.ly/3l5dqMi

Coe, R., Rauch, C. J., Kime, S., Singleton, D. and Education Endowment Foundation (2020) 'Great Teaching Toolkit: Evidence Review'. Retrieved from: www.bit.ly/3iVeekc

Hashweh, M. (1987) 'Effects of subject-matter knowledge in the teaching of biology and physics', *Teaching and Teacher Education*, 3(2), 109-120.

Hauslein, P. L., Good, R. G. and Cummins, C. L. (1992) 'Biology content cognitive structure: From science student to science teacher', *Journal of Research in Science Teaching*, 29(9), 939-964.

Newton, E. (1990) *The rocky road from actions to intentions*. Stanford, CA: Stanford University, 33-47.

Machin, S. and Murphy, S. (2011) *Improving the Impact of Teachers on Pupil Achievement in the UK: Interim Findings*. London: The Sutton Trust.

Myatt, M. (2020) *Back on Track*. Woodbridge: John Catt Educational.

Rosenthal, R. and Jacobson, L. (1968) 'Pygmalion in the classroom', *The Urban Review*, 3, 16-20.

Shulman, L. S. (1986) 'Those Who Understand: Knowledge Growth in Teaching', *Educational Researcher*, 15(2), 4-14.

Shulman, L. S. (1987) 'Knowledge and teaching: Foundations of the new reform', *Harvard Educational Review*, 57(1), 1-22.

Tharby, A. and Allison, S. (2015) *Making Every Lesson Count*. Carmarthen: Crown House Publishing.

Wiliam, D. (2019) 'Dylan Wiliam: Teaching not a research-based profession', *TES* [Online] 30 May. Retrieved from: www.bit.ly/3xe7TW7

Worth, J. and Van den Brande, J. (2020) *Teacher autonomy: how does it relate to job satisfaction and retention?* Slough: NFER.

3

DELIVERING YOUR PITCH

'We are what we repeatedly do. Excellence, then, is not an act but a habit.' - Aristotle

3.1 A scholarly culture

Preparing your pitch, as we have discussed in chapter 2, is an important component to hitting the 'sweet spot' for our explanations and models. However, no matter how much time we put into the preparation, if the culture in the classroom and wider school isn't conducive for learning this will hinder the effectiveness of being able to deliver our pitch, inevitably impacting learning. This is where the role of school leaders in establishing a scholarly culture to learning is important to support colleagues in delivering their lessons. Bridwell-Mitchell (Shafer, 2018) explored the role of culture in schools, identifying the characteristics of strong and weak cultures:

'A culture will be strong or weak depending on the interactions between the people in the organization. In a strong culture, there are many, overlapping, and cohesive interactions among all members of the organization. As a result, knowledge about the organization's distinctive character – and what it takes to thrive in it – is widely spread and reinforced. In a weak culture, sparse interactions make it difficult for people to learn the organization's culture, so its character is barely noticeable and the commitment to it is scarce or sporadic.' Bridwell-Mitchell (Shafer, 2018) identifies five key principles that underpin culture:

1. Fundamental beliefs and assumptions
2. Shared values
3. Norms
4. Patterns and behaviours
5. Tangible evidence

Devising a whole school system is the first step to developing this culture, which will look different depending on the school context. Trying to fit a whole school policy into one school just because it works in another school won't necessarily equate to success. Often the success of a whole school system is dependent on a number of factors which include colleagues understanding the intent, the consistency in how it is implemented by all staff, and regularly reviewing its impact. The role of school leaders is to ensure the 'why' of any school system is effectively communicated to colleagues and provide the necessary support to ensure the implementation is consistently applied across the school. A positive scholarly culture across the school is a crucial cog to ensure teachers are able to teach.

In recent years, I've come to appreciate the role that this plays in teaching. I used to believe that even if the school culture wasn't right, if it was right in my classroom and department then it would all be fine. Whilst there might have been a positive culture in my area, pupils have five to six lessons a day and the inconsistency in lessons across the school ultimately has an impact on pupil's attitude towards learning. It has to be a collaborative effort to see true impact.

When it comes to the classroom, it is the role of the teacher to implement the school system consistently and promote a scholarly culture in every lesson. While it is the role of the senior leaders to support colleagues in the implementation. This is supported by one of the priorities listed by the Great Teachers Toolkit (Coe, Rauch, Kime, Singleton and Education Endowment Foundation, 2020): managing the classroom to maximise opportunities to learn.

1. Managing time and resources efficiently in the classroom to maximise productivity and minimise wasted time (e.g. starts, transitions); giving clear instructions so students understand what they should be doing; using (and explicitly teaching) routines to make transitions smooth.
2. Ensuring that rules, expectations and consequences for behaviour are explicit, clear and consistently applied.
3. Preventing, anticipating and responding to potentially disruptive incidents; reinforcing positive student behaviours; signalling awareness of what is happening in the classroom and responding appropriately.

Consistency across all of the school builds a positive culture where pupils understand the expectations and the consequences when their behaviour doesn't meet them. Getting this culture right in schools is important to create the right scholarly learning environments that enable teachers to focus on explaining and modelling with precision. When pupils do display behaviour that doesn't meet the school expectations, teachers should feel empowered and supported to address this behaviour to ensure that individual pupils don't derail a carefully planned lesson. Any unnecessary distractions will inevitably affect the learning process. A shared language amongst staff is important for implementing this. For example, at The King's Leadership Academy the core values are built around ASPIRE: aspirations, self-awareness, professionalism, integrity, respect and endeavour. Whenever pupils display behaviour that doesn't meet one of these core values this provides clear feedback to pupils.

'Tom, you are not acting professionally.'
'Sarah, your current behaviour isn't respectful.'

This shared language empowers teachers and holds pupils to account.

In the classroom, we can take control and set the expectations by applying the whole school system in a consistent way. Alongside this, promoting and instilling a scholarly approach to studying your subject will support this. When teachers have an established set of routines and norms in their classroom it will provide several benefits to support instruction. This means that teachers will have to spend less time dealing with behaviour management. This in turn can reduce teacher cognitive demand, enabling them to be more responsive to pupil's learning needs. When this culture is established, this can increase teacher effectiveness and efficiency as well as providing the foundations to motivate pupils.

Sharing the value of studying our subjects and continually reminding them that they are on a journey to mastering the knowledge and skills that underpin each subject discipline is important. There are several strategies that we can use to create a scholarly learning environment.

Sam's recommendations

1. When learning something new, explain the reasons why they are studying the subject and how it is relevant to them. This is a good opportunity to share specific examples of links to the wider world. For example, when studying a novel in English, bring in a guest author to share their love for writing and the reasons why they chose to study the subject. Teachers can then refer back to them in their lessons.

2. Encourage and direct pupils to read about the subject outside of your lessons. Share examples of podcasts, newspaper articles and documentaries that will contribute towards increasing their wider understanding of the subject.

3. Show pupils the value of the subject for further study and its links to the wider world of work. Make clear links to how studying the subject can be a springboard for different professions.

4. Unpick with pupils what it means to be successful in your subject. Give clear guidance that builds on what it means to have a scholarly outlook in your school.

5. Build opportunities for debates on more controversial elements of the subject through class discussions that allow pupils to consider some of their historical beliefs of the wider concepts and processes within your subject.

6. Remind pupils that each subject discipline has its own narrative that will at times be different but equally at other times similar to other subjects. For example, developing pupil's awareness of how certain words will have different meanings. 'When exploring the role of significance in English this means we will be considering...

7. Enthuse pupils to participate in local and national subject events that support the value of studying. In geography, there are several national competitions led by The Royal Geographical Society and The Geographical Association.

8. Model academic talk and encourage pupils to think about speaking like a historian, geographer, writer and scientist.

3.2 The meet and greet

I'm sure we have all been there. A quick check of our emails as the next class arrives and within no time pupils are outside waiting for permission to come in or, depending on the school, they just wander into the room and continue with their own conversations that they have brought into your classroom from the corridors. Straight away you are on the back foot. You have to find a way to get a grip back on the start of the lesson: 'Right, stop having your own conversations please and get your equipment out ready for the lesson.'

The beginning of a lesson is important for setting the tone. You want the first few minutes of your lesson to start smoothly and pupils ready to learn from the get-go. In the early stages of my career, I learnt the hard way with a lack of structure to the beginning of my lessons. I often found myself checking emails quickly and letting pupils into the room without my full attention. Inevitably, this impacted pupils being ready to learn. I was then on the back foot. I had to find ways to claw back the start of my lesson to get pupils ready for learning. This increases the stress for you as the teacher. If only I had been taught about greeting at the door. A simple but incredibly effective technique for a calm start to the lesson.

There have been many criticisms about the meet and greet, especially around the personalised greetings that have been shared on social media. In reality, when you're teaching a 50-60 minute lesson, you can ill afford to be spending 10-15 minutes greeting at the door! However, what we can do is be at the door when pupils arrive for our lessons. It signals we are ready to welcome them into our classroom. It provides an opportunity to build positive relationships and support colleagues in a wider school strategy for smooth transitions between lessons. From past experience, when there hasn't been a smooth transition between lessons, when pupils have brought behaviours from the 'less structured' environments, such as the playground, they inevitably bring this into the classroom. When there is an unsettled start to a lesson, this has a knock-on effect for the rest of the lesson.

A study conducted by Cook et al (2018) investigated the effects of pupils' behaviour when they were greeted at the door. The study consisted of 203 students in the sixth to eighth grades (Years 7, 8 and 9). The teachers taking part in the intervention group were trained on techniques to be used when greeting pupils at the door, while other classes were provided with time to work on general behaviour management strategies. After two months, the results of the study revealed the behaviour of the pupils in the intervention group changed positively, compared to the control group which remained the same. 'Results revealed that the PGD strategy produced significant improvements in academic engaged time and reductions in disruptive behavior. Moreover, results from a social validity questionnaire indicated that teachers found the PGD strategy to be feasible, reasonable, and acceptable.' (Cook et al, 2018)

What's clear from the research is that greeting pupils will do no harm to settling the beginning of a lesson. The real challenge is the consistency in the implementation of all teachers, every lesson, every day greeting pupils so that it becomes normalised behaviour. The long-term aim is to create a settled start to the lesson so that teachers have the foundations to deliver explanation and modelling with precision.

Sam's recommendations

1. Create a calm start to the lesson by greeting pupils at the door at the beginning of the lesson.
2. Use this as an opportunity to monitor the changeover of lessons in the corridors and build relationships with pupils.
3. Have a retrieval activity ready on the board for pupils to engage with as soon as they get into the classroom.
4. Maintain a consistent approach to the beginning of the lesson. Pupils like routine.

3.3 Authenticity and credibility

Consider for a moment a time when you have been listening to a presentation and have felt the person wasn't really interested in what they were talking about.

Or, a time when you have been asked to present something that you're not completely confident with because it is somewhat detached from your expertise. This uncertainty can affect how the explanation is communicated and, inevitably, how it is received.

Consider the following everyday scenario for a moment. You have decided it is time to purchase a new television but you haven't decided which model you want. The first port of call is Currys PC World to browse the television aisle. After ten minutes of perusing around looking at the different models, you realise that without some support you're not sure which one would be best for your needs. So, you call over one of the workers for some assistance. What happens next may determine whether you leave the shop with a new television or not. The salesperson is someone you are anticipating knows their stuff. The fount of all knowledge when it comes to televisions and just the person to help you make your decision. If they couldn't answer your questions, then you wouldn't be feeling confident about their expertise and, most likely, take your custom elsewhere. On the other hand, if they live up to our expectations, we know that it will be difficult to get out of their grasp once they have sucked us in to sell a television. The art of persuasion is fundamental for business, without it many would struggle. During my A Levels I worked for McDonald's. It was normal to ask someone if they ordered a Big Mac meal without specifying whether they wanted it as a medium or large meal to say, 'Is that a large meal?' The subtle nudge towards the upgrade in all probability led to many more large meals being ordered than was originally intended.

This everyday typical scenario is just the same in our classrooms. The pupils we teach are expecting us to be the experts and the relationships that form between the teacher and their pupils is fundamental to supporting teacher explanation. Pupils need to trust us in order to believe what we tell them about our subjects and in order for them to actively listen and take on board the knowledge we share. Without this trust and air of authenticity, pupils' willingness to listen to our explanations will be hindered. Some say that teaching is an act and, in all honesty, it is. Our ability to convince the pupils we teach about our expertise in the subject they are studying is a critical cog to learning.

The role of persuasion dates back some 2000 years ago from the work of Aristotle, a Greek philosopher who shared a formula to master the art of persuasion through his work on rhetoric devices. This formula outlined by Aristotle has been used by many since then to deliver famous speeches. When it comes to teacher explanation and modelling, we can reflect on the use of three key rhetorical devices outlined by Aristotle, *ethos* (credibility), *logos* (reasons) and *pathos* (emotion). Let's explore each of them and how they can play a role in teacher explanation.

The first device, ethos, relates to your ability to convince pupils you are a credible teacher and worth listening to. In the classroom, you will inevitably have some pupils who might be more difficult to engage with than others. In option subjects like geography or history, these are the pupils who have been encouraged to take the subjects when it came to choosing their options. In a worst-case scenario – and I've experienced this at previous schools – they have been forced into doing a subject because there is no other option available to them. Motivating these pupils will be even more challenging. However, this doesn't mean it is an impossible task. This is where the art of persuasion is powerful in providing the motivation they will need to succeed in your subject. Therefore, the success of our explanations to create the foundations for learning for all pupils, irrespective of their starting point, will require the teacher to demonstrate credibility. Alongside this will be to balance our knowledge with our authority as a firm but fair teacher. Getting this balance right can take time. Generating this credibility amongst the pupils you teach doesn't mean 'letting them off' when their behaviour hasn't met the expectations or being the teacher that doesn't set homework. I remember when I was at school there was one history teacher who always told stories. Now, as we will explore later on

in this chapter, storytelling has a role in teacher explanations a
However, this is all he did. Many of my friends who had hi
would leave lessons not having put pen to paper, not having to really
themselves. They would just sit and listen to his stories. Initially, they believe
this was brilliant and gloated at the fact they did very little in lessons. However,
there came a time when the stories got boring and just sitting listening lesson
after lesson lost its appeal. In the end, pupils have more respect for teachers who
demonstrate a passion for their subject and showcase this with carefully planned
lessons that provoke thought, a degree of challenge, and the opportunity to
demonstrate what they have learnt.

John Hattie's widely recognised study on 'visible learning' indicated teacher
credibility was a vital element to learning and pupils were well-tuned to knowing
which teachers they believed could make a difference. In his meta-analyses of
practices that influence pupil achievement, teacher credibility was ranked in the
top 12 with an effect size of +0.9, double the impact on pupil motivation. When
asked about the importance of teacher credibility, Hattie said: 'If a teacher is
not perceived as credible, the students just turn off.' Prior to Hattie's research,
Thweatt and McCroskey (1998) indicated teacher credibility was an important
component of the learning process, commenting that 'the higher the credibility,
the higher the learning'.

So, what does it mean to be a credible teacher? There are four key factors that
contribute to teacher credibility: trust, competence, dynamism and immediacy.

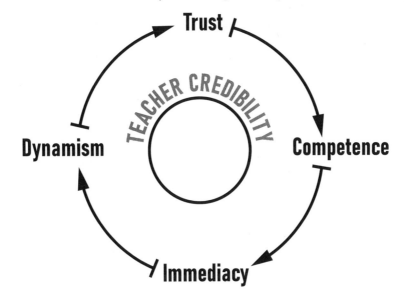

Building a trusting relationship between you and your pupils will contribute significantly to learning. When you trust someone, you will be more open to the interactions you have with them. You will pay more attention when they are speaking. You will want to listen to them. As trust builds from your first lesson with a group at the beginning of the academic year, pupils will believe what you are explaining and modelling to them.

We have already discussed the importance of teacher knowledge both in preparing your pitch but also in delivering your pitch. The role of competence in building your teacher credibility is more than just demonstrating your subject knowledge. This is where you not only demonstrate your expertise in the subject but also your competence as a teacher. Some of these might include arriving on time for the lesson, having resources all prepared, demonstrating clarity in the way you present, and when you say you're setting homework, you do. Conversely, teachers can lose their credibility through poor organisation, a lack of sincerity, not responding to pupils' questions, and a perceived lack of interest in teaching the class.

The third factor, immediacy, works by breaking down the physical and psychological barrier between you and your pupils. This will become easier when you have built trusting relationships with your pupils and the wider teaching groups. The final factor is dynamism, which is all about how you project yourself in the classroom. This is where your passion and energy for what you are teaching shines through you. When a teacher makes apologies for what is being taught this inevitably impacts the passion and dynamism of the way knowledge is presented. If we are not dynamic and passionate about what we are teaching, how can we expect pupils to be?

There are several ways we can build credibility with our pupils. Sam outlines these recommendations on the next page.

Sam's recommendations

1. Be prepared, like we discussed in chapter 2, consider any potential misconceptions/prior knowledge/questions pupils might ask during a lesson. If you can answer difficult questions, this will boost your credibility. If you can't answer a question, acknowledge this but say that you will find out an answer for them the next lesson. More importantly, follow through with this.

2. Script and practice your explanations and models to refine and execute with precision to demonstrate competence.

3. Share your love of the subject with practical examples based on your own experiences.

4. Remind pupils that you believe they can achieve the highest outcomes and your role is to provide them with the knowledge and skills to be able to achieve this.

5. Be a consistent teacher. Pupils like routine and too many unexpected changes can unsettle them.

6. Build a positive relationship with your pupils, making them believe they can be successful and achieve the highest outcomes in your subject.

7. Remind pupils as well as prepare them for times when they have struggled and not fully understand what you wanted them to learn. Tough love when it comes to addressing misconceptions is important to support pupils to achieve mastery understanding.

8. Be organised and demonstrate you are prepared to teach the class. Have the 'do now' activity ready at the beginning as pupils enter the classroom.

9. When teaching an aspect of your subject that you don't enjoy, find an angle to teach it with greater passion. Remember pupils will quickly pick up the vibe if you are not interested in what you are teaching them.

10. Get to know each of your pupils and invest time in remembering their names so that you can connect with them in lessons.

While establishing your ethos, a combination with logos will aid your explanations. Logos is all about establishing and sharing the facts and figures to formulate your discussions about the concepts and processes in the subject. When preparing your pitch, consider the facts and figures you will use to explain the concepts and processes. Providing these examples to support the core content of your subject will anchor the importance of what you explain. For example, when explaining the primary and secondary impacts of an earthquake event, sharing the key facts from a specific event like the 2012 Nepal earthquake will support pupils in understanding the severity of the primary and secondary effects. Equally, it is not about flooding pupils with a vast array of facts and figures for them to consider. Choose these wisely so that they are used to provide support for your explanations. Too many facts and figures will overload working memory and hinder the learning process.

Aristotle believed that the art of persuasion was successful when the element of emotion was considered. So, when it comes to pathos, this is all about how we can appeal to pupils' emotions. When a speaker really connects with their audience, this can be powerful. In education, knowing your pupils is important. There will be some groups where a certain example to support your explanation or model will work better compared with other groups. This is where responding to the emotions of your individual teaching groups can boost the art of your explanations and models. It is also a prime example of why there are times when the same lesson will work well with one group and not as well with another group. The dynamics of each individual teaching group make it a necessity to consider the emotions we enact when delivering our lessons.

After grappling with the art of persuasion to boost our credibility, we should also consider the role of authenticity. Take a moment to consider whether you believe you are being authentic with your pupils. Research into teacher and pupil perception suggests that our perception of authenticity is different to our pupils. When we perceive that we are acting in an authentic way, Van Petegem (2008) believed that pupils may not feel the same way. The factors that determine whether a person's actions are deemed authentic will also be different. What one pupil determines is an act of someone being authentic will not necessarily be the same as another pupil.

The research into teacher authenticity is limited with only a few studies exploring its role because quantifying the act of authenticity is challenging. In a study by Pedro De Bruyckere and Paul A. Kirschner (2016), they asked secondary school pupils what it meant when a teacher was authentic and, based on these views, they came up with four factors that contribute towards a teacher being perceived as authentic by their pupils.

1. Teachers are perceived as authentic when they know what they are talking about and can translate subject matter to the students' knowledge levels (**expertise**).
2. Second, authentic teachers are passionate about what they teach (**passion**).
3. Third, authentic teachers give students the feeling that each student and each class is different (**uniqueness**).
4. Finally, authentic teachers aren't friends with their students but have an interest in them (**distance**).

Building relationships with pupils works – both during lessons and at break and lunchtime – to boost our authenticity. When we take time to talk to pupils about their day and own interests this shows we care, as well as signalling that we are approachable and willing to take an interest in them as a person. Taking this time to build this rapport will go a long way to engaging pupils in the classroom. Reflecting on my own experiences, there have been times when some pupils have been challenging and not always receptive to listening to the input from me. This inevitably resulted in some low-level disruption and poorer outcomes when it came to applying knowledge that I had taught them. Finding the time to show pupils that you are interested in them can be a powerful tool for supporting a positive relationship between the teacher and the pupil. It could be as simple as taking an interest in their sporting activities outside of school. A quick acknowledgement of, 'I heard you played well for the school football team this week, Tom.' Taking this time to discuss their interests and finding out what they are passionate about helps to break down barriers. 'To achieve a more authentic style, teachers should use time before and after class to converse with students, allow opportunity to share experiences, and view teaching as an opportunity for dialogue between themselves and their students.' (Taylor & Francis, 2017)

In a study exploring the role of teacher authenticity, conducted by Professor Zac Johnson of California State University and Professor Sara LaBelle of Chapman University (2017), they found a positive correlation between teacher authenticity and pupil engagement: 'Open-ended data from 297 college students indicate that there are distinct behaviors employed by (in)authentic teachers. Results indicated that authentic teaching is perceived when teachers are viewed as approachable, passionate, attentive, capable, and knowledgeable.' This doesn't mean we have to reveal everything about ourselves and our private lives to pupils, but allowing them to see a little glimpse inside the life of you as a teacher can contribute towards boosting your authenticity. This is echoed in the same research study: 'Further, our findings suggest that we must attempt to be thoughtful when presenting our true self; not dishonest or antithetical to our real self, but rather cognizant of how students might perceive our actions.'

When I started at my new school in September 2020, I knew building relationships with pupils – especially Year 11 – was a key priority. When pupils wanted to know a little more about Mr Chiles, they would ask what university did I attend? What's the best country I've visited? In the classroom, this authenticity can extend to how you present your explanations and models. There might be times when you want to add an element of personal experience to your explanations. For example, I shared one story about my visit to Sri Lanka and exploring the tea plantations. Tea in Sri Lanka is served black with a sugar block and I explained the reason behind this with the teaching group. The next day one of the pupils told me they had tried tea without milk and enjoyed it. This instantly created a connection with that pupil. These personal experiences can enhance your explanations and make your knowledge more appealing to pupils.

There is no doubt that enhancing your authenticity and credibility within the classroom and wider school community will have a positive impact on creating the foundations for enhancing your explanations and models. How this looks for each individual teacher will vary depending upon our own personalities and the context of the schools we work in. Alongside the fact that the concepts of credibility and authenticity are difficult to quantify. However, as we have discussed, there are factors we can take into account that may contribute towards increasing our credibility and authenticity.

Sam's recommendations

1. Take time to build trust with your pupils so that they are more likely to believe what you tell them about your subject and better absorb the knowledge we share too.
2. Remember not to make apologies for learning about your subject. Disguise any negative thoughts. Find the motivation and passion in the more challenging parts of our subjects so that pupils are equally motivated and challenged to learn about them.
3. Keep in mind Aristotle's rhetorical devices for delivering a persuasive explanation or model through considering the ethos (credibility), logos (reasons) and pathos (emotion).

3.4 Precision

Have you ever been listening to someone and just thought, 'get to the point'? If I'm honest, I've definitely been there before. There are times when we listen to someone explaining something and think there must be a simpler way of explaining this. Or, there is that friend or colleague in the group who loves to tell you step by step the events that unfolded before they actually get to their point. Have you ever been in a situation where someone has been explaining something and soon after you have completely forgotten what they were explaining? If the explanation goes on for too long there will be a point where people's attention will start to drift. While there are times when adding context or an elaborative story can add something, when explaining difficult concepts and processes in our subject, precision can support the learning process.

Alongside the delivery is the reliance on the audience knowing what you are talking about. The person presenting may say something, a phrase, a prior event, a word that throws certain members of the group. With this in mind, knowing pupils' prior knowledge is an important factor of cognitive architecture to reduce the potential of losing your pupils.

As we discussed in chapter 1, the classroom environment can lend itself to creating all sorts of distractions. When our explanations lack precision, this will add to cognitive load and affect how pupils receive and process information into their working memory. This is particularly the case when we teach new knowledge. There has been extensive research into cognitive science and it is now widely acknowledged that our working memory capacity has a limit.

Scientists believe that our working memory capacity is low and each person's ability to process information will vary. However, it is believed that on average we are only able to process a maximum of seven different elements at any one time and this information can be lost within 30 seconds.

Sharing learning intentions

One of the first elements to being more precise in the classroom is how we turn the big picture into bite-size chunks of learning through sharing the learning intentions and breaking down what success looks like. Learning objectives often become white noise for both teachers and pupils as they have become something that teachers include because it is an expectation in a list of unhelpful 'non-negotiables'. This is echoed in the Great Teaching Toolkit:

> 'Great teachers share learning aims with their students in ways that help students to understand what success looks like. This does not mean simply writing out lesson objectives or (worse still) getting students to copy them down. Abstract statements of learning aims may be useful but are certainly not enough. To specify learning aims properly, teachers also need to have examples of the kinds of problems, tasks and questions learners will be able to do, as well as examples of work that demonstrates them, with a clear story about how and why each piece of work meets each aim.' (Coe, Rauch, Kime, Singleton and Education Endowment Foundation, 2020)

The key to successful learning objectives is engaging pupils with them to activate thought. In the past, learning objectives have been statements that have informed pupils what they will be able to do at the end of a lesson rather than what they will be learning.

To be able to explain how volcanoes are formed.
To understand why Romeo is seen as an impulsive character.

These end up becoming white noise or wallpaper in a lesson if they are not connected to the wider learning intentions or referred to during the lesson. We want to activate deeper thinking so that pupils are made to think hard about what they will be learning in the lesson or series of lessons. To create more precision and purpose to how we share the learning intentions and promote thought using challenging hypotheses or key questions. This will activate curiosity and promote thought right from the beginning of the lesson.

Ecosystems are robust, rarely influenced by external factors.
Is the impact of deforestation over-exaggerated?

Once we have shared more precise objectives, the next step is to refer to them and get pupils to continually reflect both during and after the lesson. Give them a place in the lesson and use them as a tool for pupils to reflect on what they have been learning. For example, when using key questions for the lesson, or series of lessons, this might form the basis of the application task pupils complete after acquiring the knowledge they need from your explanations and models. Ultimately, if we don't use the learning objectives after mentioning them at the beginning of the lesson, they will become a waste of time. Connecting each chunk of learning to the bigger picture is also important for pupils to understand how each layer of knowledge connects and interrelates. Continually referring to the bigger picture, the learning journey, allows pupils to see how each layer of knowledge connects and builds.

Managing prior vs new knowledge

When teachers present new content, a pupil's working memory capacity can quickly reach its limit. This creates challenges for teachers to present information in a way that doesn't hinder learning. This is something emphasised by Kirschner: 'Any instructional theory that ignores the limits of working memory when dealing with novel information or ignores the disappearance of those limits when dealing with familiar information is unlikely to be effective.'

If we know that presenting new knowledge can quickly overburden pupils' working memories, recognising prior knowledge as well as considering how we present, and the amount of information we present at any one time needs careful planning, as we discussed in chapter 2.

Once we have crafted what we want to explain, the next step is to deliver our explanations and models whilst reducing intrinsic load. Intrinsic load is connected with the difficulty of the subject content being studied. The less pupils know about something – their prior knowledge – the higher the intrinsic load. To reduce intrinsic load, we need to be aware of pupils' prior knowledge and pace the layering of new knowledge so as not to cause cognitive overload. For example, when teaching about the formation of coastal landforms, pupils need to have prior knowledge of the coastal processes before they can understand how they interact to create landforms. Without understanding these different processes, their understanding of landform formation will be fragmented.

Presenting new information in chunks that are layered over time is a fundamental cog for effective teaching and learning. It's a bit like a painter and decorator who will prepare the surface before painting, by rubbing it down, applying primer where appropriate, and then applying the top layer of paint. All of these steps, from preparation to the final application, are crucial to a professional finish. This is the same for teachers preparing and delivering their explanations. We need to consider prior knowledge our pupils possess in order to layer new knowledge to build their schema.

Aligning attention

The role of attention in the process of learning is important. Peps Mccrea emphasises this by recognising it as 'the gatekeeper of our working memory, and the ultimate currency of our classroom'. Setting a scholarly environment, as we discussed at the beginning of the chapter, is one step to aligning attention. On the whole, pupils actually prefer routine and will often behave differently if there is a sudden change from their subject norm, for example, moving to a different classroom for a lesson due to whole school activities or a lesson being covered because their usual teacher is absent. Mccrea indicates this is because routines help to 'redeploy attention', enabling pupils to spend less time thinking about the process of their learning and more time thinking about the 'content' of their learning. This supports what we discussed at the beginning of the chapter in relation to creating the foundations for scholarly learning environments that nudge towards consistent routines. This will help pupils to reduce the time spent on the process of their learning, free up working memory, and provide more time for focusing on transferring knowledge from surface to deeper level thinking.

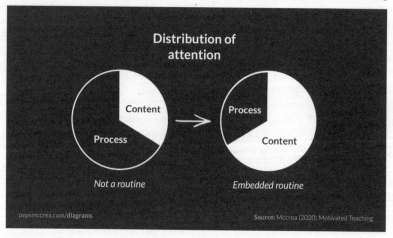

Diagram taken from Mccrea (2020)

If pupils know what to expect prior to arriving at their lesson and there are well-established routines, this means they can focus more on what they are learning. Another way we can align attention to support learning in our classroom is to ensure pupils are concentrating on our explanations and models. Stanislas Dehaene (2020) highlighted the importance of attention to learning: 'A teacher's greatest talent consists of constantly channeling and capturing children's attention in order to properly guide them.'

To support this alignment of pupils' attention we could look to implement the following strategies.

Sam's recommendations

1. Signal to pupils when you are about to explain or model something and indicate the importance of them paying attention. 'I want you to listen carefully to my explanation because you will need to use this to answer the series of questions that follow.' 'It's really important you listen to this next part because this will form the foundations for our next few lessons.'

2. Find a spot in your room to deliver your explanation. For example, this might be next to the whiteboard or when you are standing at a lectern. Make the classroom code explicit to pupils so they know that when you are in 'the spot' this is the time to make sure they are listening to you.

3. Prior to starting your explanation, insist that pupils have nothing in their hand and have their eyes on you: 'I want you all now to put your pens down and track me.'

4. Mix it up when you notice a pupil's attention is waning because of a sudden distraction in the room or something happening outside the classroom. This will amplify what they need to attend to by re-sparking their interest. Just like a comedian will read their audience and mix up their jokes to recapture the audience, there are times when teachers need to do the same in their classroom to re-align a pupil's attention to what they should be focusing on.

Worked examples and models

'Here's one I made earlier' was a familiar catchphrase used by the presenters on Blue Peter to reveal a finished product in stages. It provided a glimpse of what the finished product would look like if you followed the step-by-step guide. The use of worked examples and models in the classroom shine a light on what success looks like. It provides pupils with clarity on how they can achieve success. One of the key benefits of using worked examples is it enables pupils to focus on the solutions, rather than having to solve the problem by solely discovering the answer for themselves.

When pupils are learning something new, the pressure this applies to their working memory is far greater than when they have developed a deeper level of understanding. Without a gradual introduction, pupils can quickly be subjected to cognitive overload and this will hinder their learning. This is why the use of worked examples can be effective when pupils are beginning to develop their understanding of a new concept or process that they haven't previously studied. Using a worked example when learning something new is essentially a form of scaffolding. As pupils become more proficient in the subject, we can then begin to fade the use of worked examples. The diagram below illustrates some of the instructional techniques that can facilitate organisation and automation when learning new knowledge through reducing working memory.

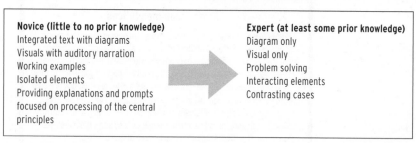

Novice (little to no prior knowledge)
Integrated text with diagrams
Visuals with auditory narration
Working examples
Isolated elements
Providing explanations and prompts
focused on processing of the central
principles

Expert (at least some prior knowledge)
Diagram only
Visual only
Problem solving
Interacting elements
Contrasting cases

To illustrate this, in a PE lesson, pupils might be learning how to dribble the ball. In the first instance, the teacher might provide a video example or demonstrate a step-by-step model. The teacher might provide a series of different videos that show examples of a series of footballers dribbling. This will provide pupils with a wider repertoire of examples to explore as they begin to practice dribbling themselves. The more practice pupils undertake, the more they will grow in confidence and improve their own dribbling of the ball. The worked example can then be faded away and replaced with the use of verbal teacher prompts. It's a bit like a child learning to ride a bike. They will need stabilisers at first and be guided until they become more confident and proficient, then they can ride independently without the stabilisers for support. There are a number of ways we can look to use worked examples in our lessons and we will explore more specific strategies that can be added to our classroom toolkit in chapter 4. For now, I would recommend teachers use worked examples and models in the following ways to deepen understanding of subjects. In chapter 4, we will expand on some of these suggestions with specific strategies that you could use in your classroom.

Sam's recommendations

1. When introducing new knowledge, use worked examples to provide pupils with an idea of what success looks like. Take the time to dissect the example so that pupils have a clear understanding of how to solve a problem.
2. Provide a partially completed example/model that pupils use to complete the final steps.
3. Create examples that connect to pupils' prior knowledge and are as streamlined as possible.
4. Develop deeper understanding by providing a range of examples. For example, if pupils are learning how to calculate percentages, a range of examples will give them an opportunity to experience different contexts.
5. Encourage pupils to compare examples. For example, if pupils are learning about the structure of musical pieces, providing several pieces of music that they can compare could help them to understand how structure varies and the impact it has.
6. As pupils' understanding begins to develop, you can begin to fade away the worked examples/models so that pupils can move from guided to independent practice. However,there may be times when you need to revisit these worked examples/models to check for understanding before adding an additional layer of knowledge as pupils move towards mastery.
7. Create a culture where pupils feel confident to discuss the worked examples/models and how they link to what they are studying to their peers. This has been referred to as the protégé effect, the idea that, when students explain study material to others, it reinforces their understanding.

3.5 Gripping stories

Picture this. It's edging closer to your usual bedtime and you have decided to put on a film or pick up a new book to read. In the blink of an eye, a few hours have passed as you have been engrossed in the power of the story that unfolds. Stories are powerful. They draw you in and make you feel like you are living it yourself. They leave you on the edge of your seat, hiding behind a blanket, laughing uncontrollably and, at times, sobbing your heart out.

Think of a time when you have made a judgement about someone and then you hear their story. How often does it change your initial view of that person? Stories have a way of hooking us in and taking us on a journey through a rollercoaster of emotions. Right from an early age, children love a story. My own two children loved a bedtime story. It became part of the nightly routine after having a bath to settle them for bed. Using stories brings lots of different benefits:

- **Engagement:** a story draws us in and makes us want to listen.
- **Inspiration:** a well-chosen carefully crafted story can inspire people to think and act differently.
- **Motivation:** as a story affects our emotional reaction, it is a powerful tool to motivate.
- **Empathy:** a story can demonstrate real empathy with our audience.
- **Connection:** because a good story is colourful, it can help us to 'get through' and not just 'give out'.
- **Credibility:** a story is an excellent way to reinforce credibility without being seen to 'blow one's trumpet'.
- **Influence:** through the emotional connection we create with the listener, the story is a perfect way to influence and persuade.
- **Likeability:** as stories are generally interesting and colourful, it can help an audience to like us (and therefore believe and trust us).

In education, the art of a story is often underestimated. This was supported by Abrahamson (2006) who said 'it is clear that storytelling may be considered foundational to the teaching profession.' Furthermore, in Daniel Willingham's first edition of *Why Don't Students Like School?*, he outlined the role stories play in our cognitive architecture: 'The human mind seems exquisitely tuned to understand and remember stories – so much so that psychologists sometimes refer to stories as "psychologically privileged," meaning that they are treated differently in memory than other types of material.'

We have discussed how the role of knowing your subject can play a significant part in both preparing and delivering your pitch. Stories are another example of how teachers can use their expertise to craft stories that capture pupils' attention. When teacher's use narratives to explain complex concepts and processes it can be powerful for learning. This is supported through a recent study conducted by Arya and Maul (2012) that involved the testing of 7th and 8th grade pupils in the US on literature based around the discoveries of Galileo or Marie Curie discoveries. The study was set up so that the two pieces of literature were similar in relation to their syntactic complexity and the vocabulary used.

Following the reading of the texts, pupil comprehension and memory was tested straight away and then a week later. The following graph illustrates the results from these tests.

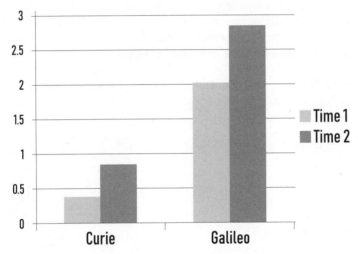

Arya and Maul concluded, 'Students exposed to the scientific discovery narrative performed significantly better on both immediate and delayed outcome measures. These findings are discussed in the context of a larger argument for the inclusion of the scientific discovery narrative in science instruction.'

Professional storytellers believe stories have some common features which consist of the following:

1. Causality: where events in a story are linked with one event triggering another.
2. Conflict: where every main character has a goal to achieve but is thrown off course by a series of challenges/obstacles.

3. Complications: where the efforts of the main character to overcome the challenges/obstacles creates a series of further challenges/obstacles to deal with.
4. Character: where each main character is interesting and is able to connect with its audience.

Willingham (2010) indicates several reasons why stories are beneficial when used effectively.

1. Stories are more interesting – people find material presented in a story format more engaging than if it is presented in expository text no matter what the topic.
2. Stories are easier to comprehend – we know the format, and that gives us a reasonable idea of what to expect.
3. Stories are easier to remember – subjects remember about 50% more from the stories than from the expository passages.

If we know that stories are powerful at grabbing people's attention, how can we use them in the classroom?

Sam's recommendations

1. Find opportunities to tell more stories in your lesson. Use of a story at the beginning of a new topic of study to set the scene. It can be a great tool to hook pupils and gain their attention to want to find out more about the topic that they will be learning. Spend time searching for interesting stories that have an edge to capture their imagination.

2. When reading a story don't rush through it. Allow pupils to immerse themselves in the story and digest what is happening. Use appropriate pause points to reflect on a section that you have read to them. Create some thought-provoking questions prior to the lesson to support this 'pause and reflect' time. Above all, remember that flying through a story because you're tight for time probably won't have the desired effect on promoting learning.

3. Share stories to promote and expose pupils to higher tier 2 and 3 vocabulary. Reading a story that contains more complex vocabulary gives pupils an opportunity to hear these words and the context in which they are used within the subject. For example, in geography, reading aloud an article from the economist on China as the world's most powerful political party will expose pupils to more sophisticated words like fortifying, engulf, strenuous and predecessor. Doug Lemov (2017) emphasises the importance of reading aloud to pupils to improve their vocabulary.

4. Provide pupils with snippets of stories for them to read and annotate. In the first instance this might be through a guided activity with pupils reading sections of a story aloud to the rest of the class.

5. As pupils' reading skills develop and vocabulary acquisition improves, create opportunities for pupils to complete independent silent reading tasks. Provide them with questions to answer as they read to allow them to complete their own 'pause and reflect' moments that you have previously modelled aloud to the class.

6. Encourage pupils to read stories outside of lessons by suggesting subject reading lists to support pupils in choosing appropriate reading for your subject. Follow this up by engaging in conversations with pupils about what they are reading and bring these into your lesson when it links well with the curriculum.

7. Use the bigger picture of your curriculum to tell a story about what they are learning. Explicitly take them on the journey with you. Articulating the curriculum story with pupils can be a powerful tool in supporting them to connect knowledge and build their schema. Sharing the learning journey at the beginning of a lesson and talking them through where they are and what they have learnt previously and will be learning can support their wider understanding of how lessons connect together. 'Last lesson we were exploring this...' 'Today we will be building on this to gain a greater understanding of the following...' This can be particularly effective in history when teachers are looking at a specific time frame of events such as the First World War.

3.6 Powerful analogies

Our subjects are awash with complex vocabulary that is unfamiliar and tricky for pupils to comprehend. When we introduce new vocabulary pupils may find it difficult to understand the concept, especially if their prior knowledge is limited. To support pupils in understanding these difficult concepts in our subject, we can use analogies. Analogies are used all the time in society but it would be counterproductive to assume that our pupils understand what they are or relate to them when they are used. Firstly, when we talk about using analogies, what do we actually mean? Glynn et al (1989) defined analogies: 'An analogy is a correspondence in some respects between concepts, principles, or formulas otherwise dissimilar. More precisely, it is a mapping between similar features of those concepts, principles, and formulas.'

Research into the use of analogies in the classroom indicates a positive contribution to learning because they can help pupils assimilate new knowledge with prior knowledge. Reflecting on your own classroom experience, I'm sure there have been many occasions where you have introduced new knowledge and quickly diagnosed that the pupils in front of you are not quite with you. There are some puzzled faces, so you have probably used some of the following phrases to formulate a connection to their prior knowledge, 'it's similar to..', 'it's like…'. When we do this, it can help pupils to grasp the new concept that we want them to understand.

Glynn et al outlined in their research that the familiar concept is referred to as the 'analog' and the unfamiliar concept the 'target'. The analog and the target will have key features and, if they share similar features, this is where an analogy can be generated.

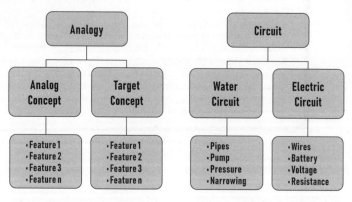

Figure 1: A conceptual representation of an analogy, with its constituent parts.

Figure 2: A conceptual representation of a water-electric circuit analogy.

Glynn et al point out that the use of analogies should encourage elaboration, which is a cognitive process that links what pupils already know with new knowledge. While we can promote elaboration by asking questions and providing personal examples, the use of analogies is a powerful tool to connect the familiar to the unfamiliar. However, while the use of analogies can enhance learning if they are not carefully planned or considered, they can equally *not* enhance learning. This is where the skill of explaining the analogy is important for it to be effective, as well as choosing suitable analogies that don't lead to further misconceptions developing. This is illustrated by the following diagram. The desired outcome from using analogies is the connection between pupils' prior knowledge and the new knowledge.

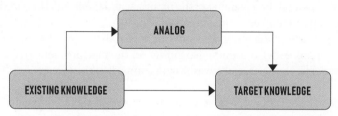

There might be times when we offer an analogy that is too simplistic and doesn't provide the required connection between the analog and target. Some pupils will require additional scaffolding when introducing the analogy. A good example of this is in geography where the connection between the earth and an egg is often used. While this can help pupils to make a connection to what is difficult for them to visualise, the complexity of the earth's structure is far greater. The structure of the egg doesn't indicate the difference between the inner and outer core. We need to elaborate on this analogy further to ensure that misconceptions don't develop.

Glynn et al (2007) proposed the 'teaching with analogies model' when using analogies in the classroom.

1. Introduce the target concept
2. Review the analogue concept
3. Identify the relevant features of target and analogue
4. Map similarities between the target and analogue
5. Indicate the limitations of the analogy
6. Draw conclusions

An example of how to explain analogies with clarity is modelled using research conducted by Stake (2007), who was looking to investigate the use of analogies to support teaching the concept of function. The following transcript provides an example of the teacher, referred to as Arturo, presenting the analogy between function and washing machine.

> **Arturo:** Before giving you more names, the function works like a kind of machine. An example could be a washing machine. A washing machine carries out a function. What is its function?
>
> **Student:** Washing!
>
> **Arturo:** What do you do? You take an article of clothing. It's dirty. You put it in the washing machine. How does it come out?
>
> **Student:** Clean.
>
> **Arturo:** Did the washing machine fulfil its function? Yes. The dirty article of clothing would be a member of the input set, and the clean article of clothing would be a member of the output set. This is what the function does. Here [he points to a diagram] we would have the dirty article of clothing. The function does what it does, depending on the machine, and arrives at the other side. In the case of a washing machine, it arrives clean.

The research indicates a positive correlation between the use of analogies and learning. To make our use of analogies effective we can look to implement the following strategies.

Explicitly model a range of analogies to support understanding of one concept where appropriate.	Plan your use of analogies during department time.	Practice explicitly modelling the use of analogies with colleagues in your department.	Explicitly explain the limitation of analogy.

Chapter summary

- If the culture in the classroom and wider school isn't conducive for learning, this will hinder the effectiveness of being able to deliver your pitch, inevitably impacting on learning.
- Establishing a scholarly culture to learning is key for school leaders to establish and support colleagues in delivering their lessons.
- A positive scholarly culture across the school is a crucial cog to ensure teachers are able to teach and pupils are able to learn.
- When there is consistency across all the schools, this builds a positive culture where pupils know the expectations and understand the consequences when their behaviour doesn't meet them.

- When teachers welcome their pupils into the classrooms, it provides an opportunity to build positive relationships and support colleagues in a wider school strategy for smooth transitions between lessons.
- Establishing a settled start to a lesson can lay the foundations to deliver explanations and models with precision.
- Without this trust and air of authenticity, pupils' willingness to listen to our explanations will be hindered.
- A trusting relationship between you and your pupils will be a positive contribution to learning.
- Connecting each chunk of learning to the bigger picture is also important for pupils to understand how each layer of knowledge connects and interrelates.
- When introducing new material to pupils it is beneficial to present these in smaller chunks that are layered over time.
- As pupils become more proficient in the subject, we can then begin to fade the use of worked examples.
- The use of narratives to explain complex concepts and processes can be powerful for learning.
- Research into the use of analogies in the classroom indicates a positive contribution to learning because they can help pupils assimilate new knowledge with prior knowledge.

Chapter resources

This resource offers a visual summary that captures the key points shared in this chapter. Having explored how we can set up our arena, prepare and present our pitch, the next chapter will provide a range of examples to model and explain through the 'Sweet Spot Toolkit'.

HTTPS://BIT.LY/SWEETSPOTCS03

References

Abrahamson, C. E. (2006) 'Motivating students through personal connections: Storytelling as pedagogy in introductory psychology'. In D. S. Dunn and S. L. Chew (Eds.), *Best practices for teaching introduction to psychology* (pp. 245-258). Mahwah, NJ: Erlbaum.

Coe, R., Rauch, C. J., Kime, S., Singleton, D. and Education Endowment Foundation (2020) 'Great Teaching Toolkit: Evidence Review'. Retrieved from: www.bit.ly/3iVeekc

Cook, C. R., Fiat, A., Larson, M., Daikos, C., Slemrod, T., Holland, E. A., Thayer, A. J. and Renshaw, T. (2018) 'Positive Greetings at the Door: Evaluation of a Low-Cost, High-Yield Proactive Classroom Management Strategy', *Journal of Positive Behaviour Interventions*, 20(3), 149-159.

De Bruyckere, P. and Kirschner, P. A. (2016) 'Authentic teachers: Student criteria perceiving authenticity of teachers', *Cogent Education*, 3(1).

Dehaene, S. (2020) *How We Learn: Why Brains Learn Better Than Any Machine...for Now*. London: Viking Press.

Glynn, S. M., Britton, B. K., Semrud-Clikeman, M. and Muth, K. D. (1989) 'Analogical reasoning and problem solving in textbooks'. In J. A. Glover, R. R. Ronning and C. R. Reynolds (Eds.), *Handbook of creativity: Assessment, theory, and research* (pp. 383-398). New York: Plenum.

Hattie, J. A. C. (2008) *Visible Learning: A Synthesis of Over 800 Meta-Analyses Relating to Achievement*. Abingdon: Routledge.

Johnson, Z. D. and LaBelle, S. (2017) 'An examination of teacher authenticity in the college classroom', *Communication Education*, 66(4), 423-439.

Lemov, D. (2017) 'why reading aloud to students is so critical to vocabulary', *Teach Like a Champion* [Blog] 25 April. Retrieved from: www.bit.ly/3gpKcos

Mccrea, P. (2020) *Motivated Teaching*. CreateSpace Independent Publishing Platform.

Shafer, L. (2018) 'What makes a good school culture?', *Harvard Graduate School of Education* [Online] 23 July. Retrieved from: www.bit.ly/3llV4qw

Stake, R. E. (2007) *Investigación con estudio de casos*. Madrid: Morata.

Taylor & Francis (2017) "Authentic' teachers are better at engaging with their students', ScienceDaily [Online] 25 May. Retrieved from: www.bit.ly/2VwFNbH

Thweatt, K. S. and McCroskey, J. C. (1998) 'The impact of teacher immediacy and misbehaviors on teacher credibility', *Communication Education*, 47(4), 348-358.

Van Petegem, K. (2008) Relationship between student, teacher, classroom characteristics and students' school wellbeing. (Unpublished doctoral dissertation Ghent University). Ghent: Ugent

Willingham, D. (2010) *Why Don't Students Like School?* San Francisco: Jossey-Bass.

4

THE SWEET SPOT TOOLKIT

'It is the supreme art of the teacher to awaken joy in creative expression and knowledge.' – Albert Einstein

When it comes to considering how we can put the research into practice, this can often be the challenging part. Educational research provides us with points to consider when preparing and delivering our explanations and models. But, it's not a one size fits all approach or a silver bullet. As classroom practitioners and school leaders, we should have the autonomy to explore how we can implement different strategies into our classrooms that utilises the research in the most effective way. There will be times when some of these strategies won't work the first time that we use them or may not be suitable for our individual school context and the pupils we teach. We should acknowledge that this is fine or implementing the strategy may look different for our own school contexts and this is something we should embrace. Alongside this, we should consider the number of new strategies we implement into our classrooms at any one time. Too many strategies can upset the routines that we have embedded. In this chapter, I will share a range of strategies that could be used in the classroom to support the delivery of your explanations and models.

First of all, let's consider what we mean by the phrase modelling. As defined by Eggen and Kauchak (2001): 'Modeling is an instructional strategy in which the teacher demonstrates a new concept or approach to learning and students learn by observing. Modeling describes the process of learning or acquiring new information, skills, or behavior through observation, rather than through direct experience or trial-and-error efforts.' Bandura (1986) believed this instructional strategy was a powerful tool in any teacher's toolkit, 'Modeling is one of the most efficient modes of learning of any new skill or knowledge'.

The first set of strategies demonstrate how you may use pre-prepared models to support pupils in their understanding of the core concepts and processes being studied.

Strategy 1: Spot the difference

There will be times when showing several different worked examples will be helpful to enable pupils to understand what excellence looks like. This is where this strategy of spotting the difference between the two worked examples could support pupils in establishing what should be included. For example, in English when pupils are studying Romeo and Juliet and developing their skills to write as a literary critic, the teacher would model two paragraphs. One paragraph which includes typical faults, such as not embedding quotations and describing literal definitions of words, while the other paragraph would model how to be a literary critic, showing pupils how to effectively apply the skills to embed quotations and analyse language with accuracy.

Exemplar 1	Exemplar 2

Strategy 2: The trader

When explaining and live modelling a concept in your subject, talking through your steps can be powerful in enabling pupils to see and understand what they need to do when they start to practice independently. Provide pupils with a series of examples that they can choose to keep or trade based on the intended success criteria. If pupils decide that they want to keep one response and trade the other, they should justify the reason for this decision.

Exemplar 1		Exemplar 2	
Keep it		Keep it	

Strategy 3: Rank order

There may be times when you want to share a tiered set of modelled responses for pupils to compare. These might be three different responses that vary in accuracy and complexity. Pupils can study each of the worked examples and decide which one best matches the intended success criteria. This could be completed as an independent or paired activity following your initial explanation and demonstration to the class. This will provide pupils with an opportunity for guided practice. For example, when pupils are studying the causes of uneven development in geography, the exemplars would provide three examples of how to explain the reasons for uneven development. Pupils would rank the responses from 1 to 3 to decide which response provides a clear explanation of a reason for uneven development. Once pupils have completed this task, the follow on could include pupils explaining a different reason for uneven development, considering the key points they had learnt from the ranking exercise.

Exemplar 1	Rank order justification
Exemplar 2	
Exemplar 3	

Strategy 4: Structure strips

Structure strips are a useful tool to provide scaffolding when pupils are applying the knowledge acquired from your explanations/models. Aligning a structure strip to the side of a pupil's book can guide them through the activity. The strip may contain a series of questions for them to consider, an outline of what to include, or key terminology. In history, when pupils are answering an essay question about the Black Death, a structure strip could be provided to support pupils in the writing process. While structure strips are a useful tool, there will be a time when removing the scaffold is important to allow pupils to apply their knowledge independently. This timescale will look different for each individual pupil and a decision to be made as pupils develop their confidence in this context as a historian. It is important that we give pupils the opportunity to try and learn from the mistakes they make. Therefore, reducing the reliance on the use of scaffolding such as structure strips is important to aiding the learning process.

Strategy 5: The 'what' and 'why'

There may be times when you want to emphasise the importance to pupils of providing clear reasoning in their answers. To begin with, you explain and model the what and why, demonstrating to pupils how to explain the points they are making. In this example below, pupils are learning about the causes and impacts of deforestation in the Malaysian rainforest.

When live modelling to pupils, stress the process:
'In this first sentence, I'm making a point about a cause of deforestation, this is important.'
'The next step to my answer is to say why this has caused deforestation.'
'Look at the connectives I've used to demonstrate that I'm doing the why part in my answer.'
'Before you start writing, consider what connectives you could use in your answer when writing your why.'

The planting of palm oil trees leads to the removal of wildlife habitats. In Malaysia, this has caused the removal of the orangutan's habitat.

....

....

The removal of trees decreases rates of transpiration.

....

....

....

Strategy 6: The annotator

This strategy could be used in a live format when presenting to pupils via a visualiser or through a pre-prepared response. For example, pupils are provided with a model response that they spend some time annotating based on the intended success criteria for the learning intentions. Or, the model can be displayed on the visualiser while you lead the discussion and annotation of the response as a whole class.

Strategy 7: Spot the mistake

Creating models that have mistakes in them can support pupils in avoiding making the mistakes when they practice applying the knowledge independently. We have already discussed the importance of preparing our pitches while taking into account and pre-empting the misconceptions pupils can have about our subjects. This is where creating examples that highlight some of these mistakes can support dispelling and preventing them from becoming embedded. For example, when pupils are studying Spanish, providing an example where there are deliberate common mistakes that pupils make when constructing sentences can help support pupils prior to their independent practice. Pupils study the example sentences and identify the mistakes before a class discussion to expand on the reasons why they are mistakes. To take this further, pupils could correct the mistakes to demonstrate understanding.

References

Bandura A. (1986) *Social foundations of thought and action: A social cognitive theory.* Englewood Cliffs, NJ: Prentice-Hall.

Eggen, P. D. and Kauchak, D. P. (2001) *Educational Psychology: Classroom Connections* (5th ed). New York: Macmillan.

5

THE SWEET SPOT ACADEMY

In this chapter, I am joined by several colleagues across different phases of education to share how they explain and model difficult concepts in their subject.

Room 5.1 Fiona Leadbeater

Art and design: Portraiture

Like all subjects, excellent modelling and explanation is vital in art and design. As the subject expert, I believe it's important to share my knowledge and experience with young people to give *all* learners the opportunity for success, not just those naturally gifted at drawing. There is a place for creative exploration, but in order to support novice learners, the direct instruction of both practical and written work is hugely beneficial to allow students to understand the properties of art materials, the way in which they can use visual qualities to enhance their work and give them confidence to use these techniques in their own creative work.

Prior to the pandemic, a regular feature of an art and design lesson would be the 'demonstration.' This would involve all pupils moving from their seats to join the art teacher around the table to see a close-up demonstration of the lesson. Physical distancing restrictions have now changed the way in which many art and design teachers work and, instead, far more regular demonstrations throughout the lesson, via a visualiser, are now common practice. In my opinion, this can only be a good thing. The demonstration is no longer limited to a single episode in the lesson and learners can now work in real time along with their teacher. Not to mention the fact that learners no longer have to leave their seat. Close-up angles of drawings can be seen easily by all learners on a far larger scale on screen, allowing teachers to really zoom in on the intricate details and learners to experience a much greater level of precision. So, what might this look like in an art classroom?

Portraiture is one area of the curriculum which is commonly taught in art and design classrooms and although every teacher will approach this differently, it's a good example to use in the context of modelling and explanation. Portraiture can be daunting for young people. It can be very easy to mess up and very obvious when it does go wrong. It's no wonder that many young people can be put off art for life and left feeling that they just 'can't draw' after attempting a portrait. But that is simply not true, everyone can draw. So, it's really important to teach this well and I believe excellent explanation and modelling are key.

Firstly, all great teachers will think about how best to chunk the learning. A portrait is complex; therefore, it makes sense to build confidence in learners by breaking the hard thing down into easier steps. To be clear, I do not mean giving learners an outline to trace, or a colouring sheet of a face to fill in. I mean explaining exactly how an artist would think when attempting to draw a portrait so there is no room for doubt about how to do this. Rather than attempting a full portrait, I might firstly teach pupils how to draw the eye. Once confident with that I would teach the nose, then the mouth. This allows learners to observe the shape and structure of these features individually without having to worry about the placement. When I'm confident learners have grasped the facial features, I would finally teach the proportions of the entire face, allowing learners to concentrate more on the measuring and features in relation to each other. I would also ensure that I was building up the complexity of the task. Perhaps using only line initially to draw, then adding in tone and texture. By breaking this down and ensuring students grasp each stage of the learning, they are far more likely to be able to build confidence and achieve success.

Now to consider my explanation. Whilst working under the visualiser, I will be constantly explaining what I'm doing with my hands to draw, where I'm looking with my eyes, and what I'm thinking inside my head. I will give students strategies to use to help them to measure, to relate things to each other and I will encourage the learners to look like an artist, perhaps using my finger to guide them around the subject matter in order to follow where my eyes are observing. I will also be checking their understanding: 'What kind of lines do I want to use here? Why?' Learners should not be just watching the demonstration passively; I encourage them to be thinking hard through my questioning. I also try to pre-empt misconceptions or common pitfalls such as mistakes with the proportion of the facial features or the shape of the head. Visually demonstrating these first hand helps students to understand why they are incorrect and avoid making these errors.

And finally, learners need time to practise. It can be tempting to keep talking, to keep explaining but it's important to give students an opportunity to demonstrate their learning. I usually go around the classroom, observing everyone's work initially, and if I've not stopped to help then students know they are on the right track. More often than not, I then find that I'm able to sit and continue my own drawing whilst students work. This allows them to have a live demo in real-time and to check back in if they need to. If my explanation and modelling have been clear enough from the outset, the support individual pupils need throughout the lesson will hopefully be minimised and learners will be far more confident about their drawing achievements.

You can follow Fiona on Twitter @TeachArtDesign.

Room 5.2 Lekha Sharma

English: Modelling writing

One of my all-time favourite lessons to teach in English is all about how to convey a mood and create an atmosphere in our writing. It's inspired by the text *Clockwork* by Phillip Pullman and it centres around description of a warm, cosy tavern nestled in the heart of a snowy town, amidst the mountains. The lesson is preceded by exploration of this rich text and immersion in this narrative, so by the time we get to modelling a suite of literary techniques to convey mood and atmosphere, the pupils are sufficiently absorbed by this beautiful text.

Modelling writing is a complex feat which involves an appreciation of the various cogs that turn in a developing writer's head. In order to begin the modelled writing, I first collect my writing tools, set out my ruled flipchart paper (that mimics the layout of the pupils' books) and position myself appropriately for the task, offering it the same attention and dedication I expect the pupils to offer their learning. Modelling of these 'attitudes' and 'approaches' to learning are just as important as the modelling of the learning itself. As an experienced writer, it's important I make these explicit to the developing writer so that they can instil these 'writing habits' into their process.

I begin by thinking out loud. 'Right, so I'm trying to convey a calm and warm mood in this tavern. Perhaps I could contrast the wintery setting with the warmth of the tavern to really emphasise the cosiness. I've got some great techniques in my toolkit, which we've created over the last few days whilst we've been deconstructing setting descriptions from lots of different authors so I'm going to keep them here so I can pick and choose. I'm going to start with some carefully selected vocabulary to describe the location…'

I continue in this way and begin to construct sentences, all the while, thinking out loud as I go along. 'I have to remember my capital letter first…' (yes, even in Year 6 because there's no harm in repeating) and construct the sentence slowly, making particular reference to joins in handwriting, punctuation used and pausing to reflect on word choice. I intentionally question mark one of the adjectives chosen and remark that 'I might come back to this one – not sure it's specific enough.' Having completed the sentence, I step back from the board and take a minute to reflect on the sentence, mirroring the 'pause and proofread' process I want my pupils to mirror. We then go on to orally rehearse the sentence as a class, proofreading to see if we have included all the relevant punctuation and to check that the sentence is grammatically correct. I tell pupils that all writers, expert or novice, are vulnerable to clumsy errors to remind them that this is a crucial stage of the composition of any text.

I continue to model, this time focusing on articulating how a writer creates cohesion between sentences by, again, thinking out loud. 'So, I've described the wintery town and the weather. Maybe now I could use the five senses to contrast the atmosphere within the tavern. I wonder what word or words I could use to really highlight that contrast? Have a talk with your partners...' At this point, I'm looking to slowly and gradually shift the cognitive load onto the pupils, first by requesting suggestions at a word level but slowly moving towards co-construction at sentence-level. As I take suggestions, we collectively stress-test the effectiveness of these on the reader, coming to mutual decisions about what would be the most effective choices as a writer. By doing this, I hope my pupils will begin to adopt an inner 'writer's voice' that naturally experiments and plays with their choices as writers until they 'hit the jackpot' as it were.

Throughout the session, my role as a teacher evolves. In the beginning I am a demonstrator and, slowly, as I 'loosen the reigns', I become co-creator and finally facilitator of the skill being taught. The 'aha' moment concluding this process, where pupils are fully-fledged authors experimenting, manipulating and playing with words, sentences and techniques and debating their effectiveness is a thing of beauty! As the year progresses, my role as demonstrator of skill shifts largely to facilitator of practice of skill. Seeing pupil flourish as writers throughout the year never fails to remind me of the undeniable importance of intentional and consistent modelling in the process of learning.

You can follow Lekha on Twitter @teacherfeature2.

Room 5.3 Richard Clutterbuck

Religious education: The problem of evil and suffering

This is one of my favourite parts of the curriculum to teach. It never fails to deliver discussion, disagreement, digressions, wild leaps of logic and those wonderful light-bulb moments when the pupil, after several moments of thought, responds to a question with, 'Sir, so if God is all-powerful, and if God is...' without even finishing their sentence because they have made the necessary links in their head. You can see the dimmer switch spinning clockwise as their thoughts are illuminated with the sudden realisation of what had previously been beyond them. It's a topic for pupils to chase each other and me down every philosophic and ethical rabbit hole imaginable. And herein lies my problem, and it's a perennial problem. As I build up the layers of knowledge necessary to understand the problem, as I reference the 'nature of God' and concepts of 'evil' and 'suffering'. As I layer them together, with the attributes and essence of God juxtaposed with the origins of evil, I consider various religious responses to the framing of the arguments. For the pupils, the sheer volume and weight of all relevant parts needed to understand the problem of evil (and suffering, for the sake of argument) can be – and usually is – overwhelming.

Whether we're framing spoken arguments or composing our written responses, the results from the pupils often fall short of my expectations. Why do I get such narrow, superficial responses from the pupils once I've taken away my scaffolds? Why do they get so muddled when previously they we able to state certain parts of the argument so clearly and eloquently?

As I wrote earlier, it's a perennial problem. No matter how clear my explanations and instructions, how regular my checking for understanding, how structured and well-paced my live modelling, I am still left with a sense of frustration that a topic which began so well has not lived up to my expectations. I feel a sense of guilt that I can't take all of the pupils right through to the end and produce spoken and written responses to match their early flair. And this is my problem with the problem of evil. That is, until recently. Knowing that the problem I have is *my* problem and not the pupils, I have discovered the missing piece of the pedagogical jigsaw. It provides the links between my explanations and modelling; it does the heavy lifting of the different facets of knowledge the pupils carry into their responses and it allows me and the pupils to zoom in and out of the topic so that we can all see what knowledge is required and where it is coming from. Building on the work of Oliver Caviglioli, I have followed David Goodwin's blogging on graphic organisers and word diagrams.

These, for me, are the missing pieces of the jigsaw I have needed to ensure that pupils are able to produce the written and verbal responses I know they are capable of. My use of graphic organisers and word diagrams, alongside my explanations, checking, modelling, scaffolding and retrieval practice, have had a profound effect on my teaching of the problem of evil, and more importantly, the pupils' responses to the problem.

Quite simply, the undiagnosed problem was cognitive load. Despite my best efforts, the leap I made from imparting the knowledge to expecting the pupils to frame it all in clear, logical, balanced responses was too much. They just couldn't remember it all in the right sequences. My use of graphic organisers and word diagrams now allows the pupils to walk easily across the gap I expected them to leap across. Consequently, the pupils' responses (both verbal and written) now match, if not exceed, their early flair and promise. And my guilt has gone!

The beauty of a graphic organiser is that it provides a focal point for my initial explanations, it allows me to zoom in to the detail of the point I am explaining but also allows me to zoom out so that the pupils can see where this particular piece of knowledge sits in relations to the overall problem. Pupils can see the path that we are navigating through the topic but, at any moment, can drill down into the key parts of the argument.

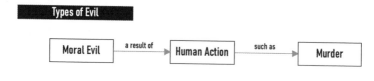

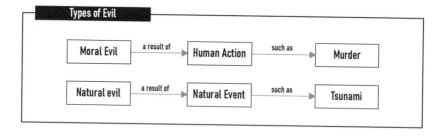

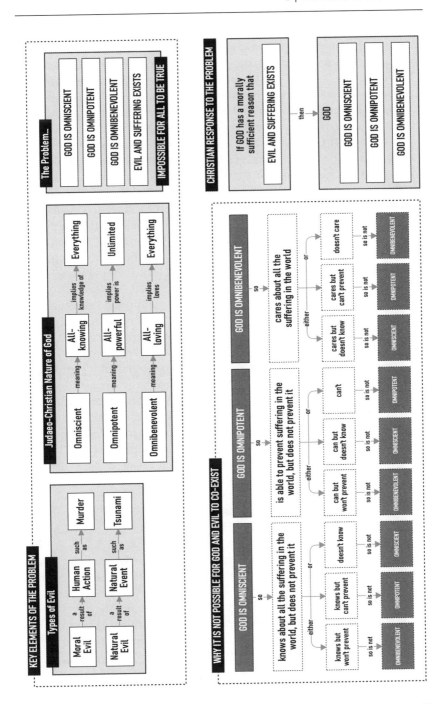

The effective use of graphic organisers, for me, is in the reveal. Showing pupils the whole graphic organiser too early can give them 'map shock', as David Goodwin calls the cognitive overload pupils experience. So, where I have created a graphic organiser in PowerPoint, I use the animation tools extensively, otherwise I will draw the map, section by section on the board, using my usual pedagogy around it to ensure understanding. PowerPoint's ability to zoom in and out is a lifesaver and is worth the time transforming a graphic organiser from notes on to a slide. Having the whole map but being able to zoom in and out avoids pupils being overloaded with information and losing their place on the organiser, while also allowing me to show them the whole picture and the key specifics. Graphic organisers have practical uses beyond aiding my explanations and modelling, I will give them to pupils partially completed so they can fill in the missing parts as part of our retrieval practice routines. According to Goodwin and Caviglioli (2021), graphic organisers can be used as 'an external memory field... distributing the cognition'. And this is evident to me from the increased accuracy of answers from pupils when I am checking that they understand.

Where the graphic organiser I use has its limitations when I need pupils to provide a response to a GCSE question, either written or verbal, a statement such as 'all suffering can be used to show God's love – discuss' can help expose those limitations. The graphic organiser shows how the knowledge sits together but it does not help the pupils frame a suitable response. Initially, I tried to use the graphic organiser as a tool for helping to construct answers but I ended up changing the diagram so much that starting with a blank sheet of paper was far more efficient. Again, I have gone to my gurus Oliver Caviglioli and David Goodwin for the answers and I have developed word diagrams to aid the pupils written and verbal responses. Similar to graphic organisers, they reveal, through concepts and verbs, the mental structure of written responses but make them visible on the page or whiteboard. They sit somewhere between kernel sentences and graphic organisers, showing how sentences build up into structured responses but avoids having too many connections and losing the focus of the response.

My graphic organiser may give the pupil some clue as to how to answer some parts of the example question above but what the pupils really need is a diagram that can support them in structuring their answers. I use the word diagrams to construct model answers with the pupils. Under the visualiser I will show them how to use the diagram, tracing my finger from concept to concept across the verbs, writing down the sentences as I go. The diagram lessens the cognitive load for the pupils and allows them to understand what I am thinking in my head as I model the answer for them. Handing the pupils the same diagram and getting them to enact the process with me is extremely useful and is a plain steal by me from Oliver Caviglioli's Corsica exercise (2021).

The following graphics shows the whole word diagram and when the time comes for the pupils to write a written response independently, this is the final piece of scaffolding I will leave with them. I also insist they use it, and in the same way I did when I live modelled earlier written responses for them. Helping pupils get underway or start the next part of their response is made far easier with the aid of the map. I will show them where to place their finger and say the words as they move along the lines. Once they have rehearsed this a few times, they are able to use the method with the map to construct their answers.

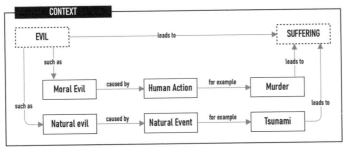

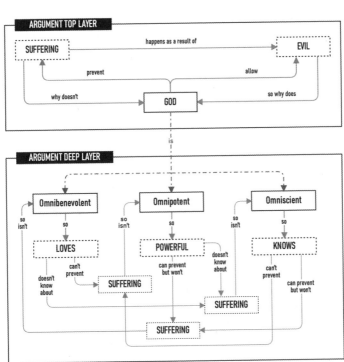

Until the pupils know the content (in other words, have seated the knowledge in their long-term memories), graphic organisers and word diagram act as an external extension of their memory. The pupils and I can focus on the nuances of the topic knowing that cognitive load will be kept in check and our working memories are free to understand how we move from types of evil, to the nature of God, to critiquing God's nature, to the relevant religious response. So, how do I know that I have fixed the problem I have with the problem of evil? Well, the topic still generates heated debate, discussion, and those light-bulb moments I mentioned at the beginning. It is the very essence of why I love religious studies. With the additional use of graphic organisers and word diagrams alongside my existing pedagogy, the quality of writing from the assessments is of a much higher standard across classes and pupils' recall of key concepts and arguments is secure.

Graphic organisers and word diagrams are a revelation for me and my teaching, but I am careful not to use them in isolation. They aren't magic bullets for me yet, they are the missing pieces of the jigsaw that were causing me frustration with a topic that I love to teach. What do I need to do next? Well, my ambition is to teach the pupils how to construct the graphic organisers and word diagrams themselves. I have seen the success David Goodwin has enjoyed and that for me is the next level. The trial and error has begun, but I will get there.

You can follow Richard on Twitter @rclutterbuckED.

Room 5.4 Kyle Graham

History: Modelling significance in essay writing

History is a subject that requires extensive modelling in order to show students how to write in an academic and professional manner. There are many assumptions from those outside of the subject that there are many similarities with English and while there are some parallels, there are many areas in which the subjects diverge as well. As a history teacher with a history degree, you have to be aware that you are the expert in the room and showing students how you think and write can only expose them to the kind of high-level processing that a university graduate would have. This can only help in taking them to the next level of their history education.

Let's look at a study of significance as an example. Significance is one of our key concepts in history and is a fundamental part of the subject right the way through to PhD level. If you cannot debate or explain what makes an event significant, you will struggle with any type of question or thinking around history as, ultimately, history is a study of significance. The issue, of course, is that significance is highly objective. This means that what one student says is highly significant could be contested by another student. It's those skills that we need to equip students with in order to be able to get these complex and evaluative ideas down on paper.

I think there are several ways in which we can guide significance thinking in the classroom in a way that ultimately builds up to an excellent piece of historical writing. We're going to assume that the early legwork and knowledge building is done here, because building a core baseline of knowledge is something that could be written extensively about in its own right. There are several layers to building up significance thinking from this point – ultimately, you want students to be able to compare and contrast events and individuals and debate which are more significant than others and have strong rationale for their thinking that correlates well when pen is put to paper.

Step 1: Formulating the success criteria

This is the first step to significance. How are students going to judge the significance of an event if they have not first considered the success criteria for what would make an event significant? Let's get that down first and involve students in the process. What makes an event, discovery or individual significant? Draft ideas out on the board with them and then get the students to think about which of these ideas have greater weighting. Is it more significant that a medical idea was correct or that it influenced people for a long time, despite being wrong? Likewise, is accuracy important if nobody knew about the idea? Encourage students to discuss and debate this but also encourage them to come up with their own conclusions. It's okay for different students to give different weighting to different things. Remember, it is subjective. Do, however, play devil's advocate and challenge their thinking, offering alternative viewpoints.

I would always recommend splitting any study of significance into short and long-term significance as it is excellent academic history to look at how an individual's significance may wax and wane with the flow of time.

Step 2: Applying the success criteria

Now that students have decided the baseline for what makes events significant, they have to apply this to the topic being studied. What makes an individual such as Louis Pasteur significant? How significant? It is important to model language here, perhaps by giving students a scale of significance using high-level academic diction. Phrases such as 'of the utmost significance' reads much better than 'very significant' so encourage your students to use that and correct them when they don't. Ask students if significance was greater in the long term or the short term and why? What events did that discovery or event lead to? Does that make it more or less significant? Is the individual regarded as significant in the wider world? Why may this be? Introduce a little comparison here – which is more significant and why? Again, you can discuss this as a class but do get students to write their ideas down here as well. Share these ideas with the class before the next step.

Step 3: The writing

This is where the major element of modelling comes into play. The increased use and appreciation of visualisers is well written about by now, and I absolutely agree that they are key to modelling in particular. So, let's do a class write then, as this way you can challenge thought like you have been so far, whilst also upgrading language and demonstrating your thinking. The alternative, of course, is you could write an answer and explain your rationale as you go along, or ask students why you have done certain things. For this example, let's say it's a class write.

Firstly, explain the structure that you want. A paragraph on short-term significance and a paragraph on longer term significance, followed by a conclusion on overall significance. Ask students to write this down with you and annotate it as you go along. You want your opening sentence to be dynamic – a DOS (dynamic opening sentence). Ask students to come up with one and feed them back and get the class (with your prompting) to choose the best one. Ask students to improve on language if need be. Prompt thoughts on what comes next and bounce ideas around the class. Think of questions like: 'What's a better way of phrasing that?', 'Is there more specific factual information we could include there to make that sound even better?', 'What evidence would support that point really well?'

Always challenge explanations and knowledge to be as specific as possible. The age-old idea is to ask why three times in order to get the best explanation, and that works well when asking students to explain significance as well. Feel free to ask 'does anybody disagree with that?' about points and encourage them to debate. By the end students should have an answer in their book that is highly academic and annotated with rationale such as specific factual information, explanation of what this event led to, long-term/short-term impact, consideration of alternative viewpoints and so on.

The natural follow up to a task like this is to get students to write their own, but on a different individual/event, referring back to the well designed and thought-out structure and language that was placed into your work. There is no real substitute for students seeing the thinking of a university-level subject expert, and by the end of a lesson like this they will, hopefully, have been incredibly challenged and supported in moving their academic writing to a new level.

You can follow Kyle on Twitter @KTG_1990.

Room 5.5 Kate Jones

History: Reflecting on modelling

I recall learning about the powerful impact modelling can have in the classroom. I read about this in various educational books and blogs but I struggled to implement it effectively in my own classroom. On reflection, I should have asked colleagues for advice on how they use this classroom strategy in lessons with their students. Learning from others is often underrated and something we don't do enough of it in schools – it can be a form of low cost, low effort but high impact professional development.

The first error I made in terms of modelling – and this might seem bizarre but I know other teachers have done the same – was to show 'what a good one looks like' *after* students have completed the task. This was a mistake; I should have shared, discussed and explored the example prior to students completing the task. I think as teachers we can be reluctant to do so because we feel like we are revealing the answers to students before they have even attempted it themselves, but that is exactly what we should be doing.

During an A Level lesson, I was providing whole-class feedback to my students about a recent extended essay they had completed. Although I had provided advice and guidance prior to them writing their essays about how they structure their answers, it was clear they hadn't grasped this. I decided to show the class exemplar answers. These were provided by the examination board and varied in terms of marks and grades but were generally high. We read through the essays together, with my comments as the class made annotations and notes. The students told me the lesson was very helpful and one student remarked, I wish I had seen that before I submitted my essay! I realised I should have gone through this process before they had attempted the essay question, not afterwards. This is something I now do with my exam classes and it is clear it has a big impact on helping students understand the required structure, focus, assessment objectives and the amount of necessary content. Not all students master this immediately, we wouldn't expect them to, but it does help them master it sooner rather than later.

It is important that all examples used are anonymised. If they are provided by an exam board then they are automatically anonymised and the student whose work is being discussed is completely removed from the school context. However, if you decide to share an example from another class or previous cohort then, again, it is important to anonymise. Students often don't mind their work being shared with their peers; they can even like it (when shared in a positive light) but this isn't the main issue. When a class are studying the work completed by another student from their school, questions will arise as to whose work it is. They often try to recognise the handwriting or make guesses about who it could be. The focus should be on the work being shared, not the student. That can become a distraction.

Teachers have been known to write model answers to help students understand the requirements in terms of structure, focus and content, but this can be problematic. When students read an essay written by the teacher they automatically think: 'This was written by my teacher who is an expert in this subject so no wonder it's so good!' The class may also not wish to critique the work because they can feel that they are insulting their teacher and perhaps feel that they may get in trouble. In contrast to this, some students may desperately want to find errors and areas for improvement because it is the teacher! Students can take satisfaction in teachers making mistakes, although we are only human, it happens. My advice, if you are writing an example to share with the class, is to anonymise it and not say that you wrote it. Anonymising work should become the norm so that students will eventually realise not to ask who completed the work because the teacher won't discuss that.

Modelling, demonstrating and sharing exemplars has the potential to be a very effective teaching and learning strategy to support learners however, it is not immune from being lethally mutated as many other strategies in education have been. The key is to continually reflect on this practice, talk to and learn from others and evaluate the impact on student progress and long-term learning.

You can follow Kate on Twitter @KateJones_teach.

Room 5.6 Alistair Hamill

Geography: The general circulation of the atmosphere

It's only as I have become more active on Twitter over the past few years that I have realised that, if there is one thing sure to cause geography teachers to break out into a cold sweat, it's the prospect of teaching the General Circulation of the Atmosphere to their class (indeed, the capitalisation feels entirely appropriate for this is indeed Very Much A Big Thing for many geography teachers).

In some senses, the reaction was a bit of a surprise to me. I actually love teaching this topic. Yes, it's tough, but it's also one of those topics where you literally get to see the 'light-bulb' moments happening in your class. However, I do appreciate the challenges of teaching it. It is a complex and cognitively demanding topic than can easily lead to cognitive overload. It is a topic that is easy for pupils to make mistakes on that – if not spotted and quickly corrected – can result in embedded misconceptions that are hard to shift and compromise subsequent learning. Bringing a whole GCSE class with you as you go through your explanation is challenging; some will get it more quickly than others, but you can't leave any pupil behind. In my decades as a classroom teacher, I've faced my fair share of those challenges. But I have found an approach to teaching that has helped me meet them and brought me to a place where this is one of my favourite set of lessons in the whole topic of atmosphere.

The underlying principles

The concept of schema building is helpful when thinking about teaching the general circulation of the atmosphere, as it is a topic that draws together an evolving understanding of this particular geography content in an applied way. Enser and Enser (2020, p. 20) define a schema as an '...architecture of the mind in which memory and understanding is constructed and, perhaps even more importantly, reconstructed'. It is this applied, ongoing sense-making concept that I have found very helpful in planning to teach this topic. I need carefully to plan what prior learning I need to activate with the pupils, and then to support and scaffold the work for them as they go through the iterative process of integrating this new understanding into their evolving schema.

Activate the key prior learning

I begin by clearly bringing to mind core concepts of the topic of atmosphere that I introduce right at the start of this whole theme and weave throughout. In this case they are:

- The atmosphere acts to redress imbalance, for example:
  - Air moves from high pressure to low pressure (driven by what is called the pressure gradient force).
  - Heat moves from warmer areas to colder areas. (The atmospheric equivalent of the cry heard in many homes around the country as kids leave the room, 'Shut the door, you're letting the heat out!' Everyday comparisons like this help make the abstract ideas more concrete.)
- Rising air results in lower air pressure and falling air in higher air pressure at the surface (pressure is the weight of the air pressing down on the ground surface).

This is not just to bring to mind relevant prior ideas before new ideas are introduced – it's more fundamental than that. The way we will learn this topic will be to take these core concepts and carefully and explicitly apply them.

Application via small steps and key questions

Once these core concepts have been brought to mind, I then break down the explanation into very small steps which are taught through carefully planned questions to get them to apply the concepts. I get them to rule out a horizontal line on a page and we mark on the key latitudes (0°, 30°, 60°, 90°) of a cross section view through the atmosphere from the North Pole to the South Pole, and I draw a similar line at the front on the board (supporting cognitive load by using an external memory field like a diagram is key in helping keep the pupils with me as we move through).

Then comes the series of key questions: 'Is it warmer at the equator or poles? Does warm air rise or fall?' As these are simple questions, choral answers from the whole class do the job. Then we add an 'up arrow' at 0° on our line to represent the warm rising air at the equator. Next, another question based on prior learning: 'Does rising air give higher or lower pressure at the surface?' I get the pupils to think about this, then they all vote (thumbs up or down). This allows me to instantly see how effectively they've all been able to apply this core concept. If their application is patchy then this will prompt me to recap. At this stage, it is vital that everyone in the class grasps these first steps before we all move on.

We then connect back to some more prior knowledge they will have (convection cells) as we complete the arrows as shown in the diagram. Then, another question: 'Does falling air give high or low pressure?' This is, clearly, a very similar question to the one I've just asked and deliberately so. By carefully planning questions that apply the same core concepts over and over again, I support the pupils in the application of their thinking. The procedures we follow throughout in question are similar, but the content changes slightly. This manages the cognitive load, keeping the pupils focused on the content I want them to think about. We then mark high pressure at 30° on the diagram.

At this point, we are at a key stage in the explanation. This is the first time the pupils will have met pressure imbalance in the exercise. So, I say this: 'We now have a pressure imbalance – high pressure at 30° N/S and low pressure at the equator. The atmosphere acts to redress this imbalance. Draw a line onto the diagram to show how that is done.' This is vital as a diagnostic tool for me. I can see those who get it and those who are struggling a bit more so that I can intervene in the moment to help them, but it's also a vital stage in the generative learning process for the pupils. They need to think; they need to apply. It's that application process that will be key in helping the pupils reconstruct meaning as their schemas evolve.

Once we have completed this and I'm happy that everyone has understood, we move to the poles, again with a series of key questions that are answered via whole class choral response.

'If it's hot at the equator, at the poles it's…?' I ask, to answers of 'cold'.
'If warm air rises, cold air…?' I ask, to answers of 'falls'.
'If rising air gives low pressures, falling air gives…?' I ask, to answers of 'higher pressure'.
'If air moves towards low pressure, at high pressure it moves…?' I ask, to answers of 'away'.
'Good! Okay, mark that onto your diagram with an arrow.'

The approach I take here very deliberately echoes and mirrors what we have just done. Again, my goal is to make the procedures we follow and the questions I ask sufficiently similar that the pupils can answer them and grow in confidence, but you may notice I am removing the scaffolding a bit, giving just a little bit more independence to the pupils as we proceed through. As we move through the final latitudes to be covered, we follow a very similar path – keeping the same procedural approach (to help manage the cognitive load) whilst slowly and carefully reducing the scaffolding in the questions I ask.

Once we have completed the entire diagram, I give the pupils a little bit of thinking time to review what they have just done and ask any questions they may have. Then they do it all again on a blank page. This time, I will ask the key questions again but I don't draw it at the front and I allow the pupils to move at their own pace through the task, not from memory of what we have just drawn but by applying their developing understanding. This allows me to see the pupils who are confident, for whom the schema connections are being well made, and those who are struggling a bit more who I can give a little bit more support, helping clarify any parts they are struggling to connect. The support is there but the scaffolding is reduced a bit, giving pupils more and more confidence that they can do this by themselves.

Finally, it's time for their homework. 'We're going to do retrieval practice on this next lesson, but your homework is not to learn this off by heart! I'll guide you through again, asking those key questions, and you will apply your understanding.' And, over the years, I've found that the success rate in the next few lessons, as we consolidate this learning, has been very high. The key for them, every time they reproduce the diagram, is not to try to remember what the diagram looks like but to reconstruct it from first principles, asking themselves the questions I first asked, thus strengthening the connections of understanding in their schema.

Small steps, similar procedures throughout, carefully planned questions, scaffolding that is gradually reduced, diagnostic questions throughout to identify and address misconceptions as they arise, and questioning that gets the pupils to think hard about what they are doing. Through this approach, carefully crafted over the years, I have the privilege of seeing light-bulb moments all over the classroom. And, as any teacher will know, those moments are always A Very Enjoyable Thing Indeed, very much deserving of a capitalisation treatment, I'm sure you would agree.

You can follow Alistair on Twitter @Icgeography.

Room 5.7 Emma Turner

Mathematics: Avoiding common misconceptions in the initial teaching of early fractions

A sound understanding of fractions forms part of the foundations of Key Stage 2 mathematics but begins to be developed from Early Years Foundation Stage and through Key Stage 1. Fractions is a relatively straightforward concept. It is one which is in the daily lived experience of young children through activities such as sharing and halving. However, within the specific teaching of fractions within their mathematics experiences at school, there are lots of potential misconceptions that can lead to confusion in younger learners. This section aims to outline what some of those misconceptions might be and how these can be avoided through practical activity and sound teacher exploration of the concepts. Good understanding of fractions is pivotal to success in Key Stage 2, as the bulk of work from Year 4 onwards relies upon a solid foundation in early fractions.

Fractions is often referred to as part of 'FDPRP', which stands for fractions, decimals, percentages, ratio and proportion. Fractions is first in this acronym as without it the rest are difficult to access or understand. The bulk of upper Key Stage 2 number consists of elements of FDPRP and so children ideally need to enter Key Stage 2 already fluent and fully conversant in the basics of the concept, just as they would ideally enter fully conversant with the four operations, place value and number facts. To ensure fractions are introduced effectively and successfully linked to future images and teaching approaches, the following section outlines some key teaching points within progression in fractions.

Common misconceptions in early fractions

The first potential misconception is around equipartitioning.

- **Equipartitioning and 'the bigger half'**

Equipartitioning is the demonstration of a fraction being a whole or set cut into *equal* parts. The misunderstanding that there is somehow a 'bigger half' is a common one as this links to children's direct experience, such as if a cake is not cut into two equal parts, it may have been referred to as having a 'bigger half'. Children need to explore and have modelled for them, fractions which do and don't represent equipartitioning.

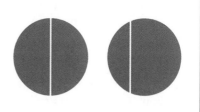

- Natural experience – breaking, sharing
- Key teaching point is 'equipartitioning'
- Needs modelling with 'wrong' and 'right'
- Pupils need opportunities to discuss why fractions representations are or aren't correct

- **Notation**

Very often, exploration of the notation for fractions is overlooked. When questioned in Key Stage 2 why a ½ or ¾ is represented as they are, many children cannot articulate what the function of each part (including the line) in the fractions means. Children should ideally be taught the appropriate vocabulary of numerator and denominator as soon as possible in their fractions experience and know the function of each.

The denominator (bottom number) is the total number of equal groups a whole or set has been divided into. The numerator is the (top) number of those total sets you are referring to within a specific fraction, e.g. ¾ would be splitting a whole or quantity into four equal groups or pieces and then highlighting or referring to three of those groups. It is *not* correct to say that 'the larger number goes at the bottom', as when children encounter improper fractions later in their maths experience, e.g. ⁵⁄₂ or ⁴⁄₃ then this rule becomes a 'false rule' that no longer applies. Practical experience of building fractions using counters or cubes or matching pictures of fractions to their notation is a key experience at this stage.

- **Using an ordinal link**

When using fractions and 'cutting' wholes into fractions of different sizes, it can turn children's thinking about number on its head. This because ¼ is smaller than ⅓ but the denominator of 4 is greater than that of the 3 in ⅓. This can be confusing for some children as they continue to use an ordinal link to compare the relative size of fractions, thus assuming that ¼ is worth more than ⅓ because '4 is more than 3'. This is where practical experience is imperative. Children need the experience of seeing that the more pieces you cut a whole into, the smaller the pieces become. Questions such as, 'Would you rather have ¹⁄₁₀ or ⅓ of your favourite cake?' can also help to move away from an over reliance on an ordinal link.

However, it is incorrect to use the rule of 'the bigger the denominator, the smaller the fraction' as this only works when comparing unit fractions (fractions with a numerator of 1). If you compared ⁵⁰⁄₁₀₀ this is still more than ⅓, even though the denominator is significantly larger. This is another 'false rule' which if taught in early fractions can lead to great confusion later on. Using ordering activities (beginning initially with unit fractions and then integrating some other simple fractions such as ¾) can, when supported with practical resources and exploration, help to deconstruct the reliance on an ordinal link.

It is an important point to note too that initially, when exploring the comparison of fractions, the same size equipment is used. You can see from the following graphic that ½, ¼ and ⅛ are much easier to compare in size in the top row of circles, whereas the language associated with ordering fractions would become much more confusing in the bottom row where, in 1/8, each eighth section is actually larger than the ¼ in the circle to the left. Careful use of resources and modelling is crucial at this point to support children's early understanding of the representation of fractions and their relative size.

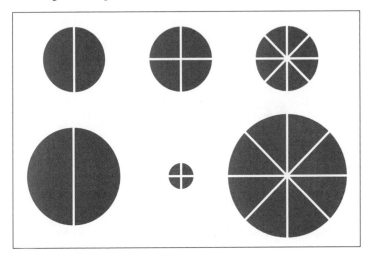

- **Quantification**

This is where children may represent the quantity of a fraction incorrectly with counters or other equipment, e.g. in the following graphic, figure A is incorrect and figure B shows the correct representation of ¼. Many children misunderstand quantification and apply the logic that ¼ is represented as 1 counter over 4 counters rather than seeing it as a fraction of 1 out of 4.

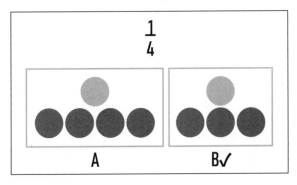

Practical exploration and mapping/matching of the correct representation with the notation is key at this point. By using double-sided counters in a line and then 'flipping' one of them in the linear arrangement prior to moving them into the vertical arrangement as above, can help to unpick this misconception. In the picture below, four blue counters have been laid out then one 'flipped' to red before arranging in the vertical arrangement above.

- **Reconstituting**

Another area of misunderstanding within early fractions is that of not recognising that fractions can be reconstituted, e.g. if ¼ of a circle is red, then understanding that ¾ is not red. It is a little like not recognising that there are three numbers in a number fact or bond. In the number bond 7 + 3 = 10 there are three numbers: 7, 3 and 10. Within the fraction of ¼ there are 3 values: 1/4, ¾ and the whole. Children need plenty of experience reconstituting fractions as well as finding simple fractions if they are to fully understand their associated concepts and values.

Labelling shapes and diagrams or creating their own fractions with counters as above in the quantification section can help to secure the three parts of the reconstituting. Children need opportunities to describe and articulate what each section of their representations look like at this point. By doing this early on with shape and simple unit fractions, this will lead to secure foundations for work on fractions of number and solving problems within fractions, as well as within ratio and proportion.

- **Language and vocabulary**

There are many more new words and terms to learn within the concept of fractions, many of which can appear confusing, especially when linked with ordinal language, e.g. a child may see a 'fifth' only as 'the fifth' so may not recognise that all other sections in a fifths fraction diagram are also fifths. The following diagram shows the misconception that ordinal language can be applied to fractions. It is especially confusing when you think that this particular diagram also contains the ordinal language of 'third' when it is representing fifths.

Modelling using clear, consistent transferable diagrams is key at the point of learning new language around fractions. Children need a chance to practise the speaking and use of fraction vocabulary, as well as just hearing or reading it. By encouraging them to talk about the diagrams you use and draw during modelling, misconceptions and misapplications are much easier to pick up.

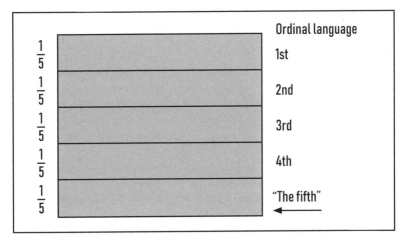

Key points

- Understanding potential misconceptions within fractions is key to effective modelling and scaffolding within fractions.
- Children's everyday use or experience of fractions may include misconceptions such as 'the bigger half'.
- Keeping diagrams and models equal in size and simple in design helps to demonstrate key concepts.
- Practical exploration with concrete apparatus is a key step in the development of understanding.
- Ordinal language can be misapplied to fractions and will need explaining and exploring.
- Modelling and explanation should be designed to explore and unpick the common misconceptions.

You can follow Emma on Twitter @Emma_Turner75.

Room 5.8 Avril Purchon

English literature: Conscious (de)construction of conceptualised thought

English literature as a discipline is multifaceted. There are a multitude of ways to interpret literature and each interpretation varies wildly dependent on each reader's viewpoint and perspective. An individual's interpretation of a text could be rooted in geographical location, gender, sexuality, race, religion – none of which may be what was intended at its conception.

In order to produce unique, concise, clear thought, students must first be able to recall and understand a text, applying their own knowledge of context and writer's intentions before teasing out those golden threads of thought which form a response to any given question. Once this foundation has been created, it is possible to discuss, debate and grapple with the big themes and concepts underpinning a text's existence and pull together an individualised response, personal to each student and driven by knowledge.

This multifaceted nature of literature is what makes consciously teaching students how to approach an essay from a root concept so tricky. Theoretically, with an infinite number of words and an infinite number of minutes, students would come up with an infinite number of concepts or ideas around their text. Inevitably, however, they frequently seem to come up with the same two or three ideas, worded ever so slightly differently in two or three paragraphs. So how do we consciously construct unique conceptualised thought in English at Key Stage 3 and beyond? The idea itself is straightforward – come up with your own opinion based on what you have just read. It is rarely so easy. In order to simplify the process, there are a number of steps which can be taken to model, deconstruct then reconstruct conscious knowledge-driven responses.

Modelling independent thought

Throughout a lesson there are many questions posed to students. In order to foster a culture of open discussion first there must be a safe space in which to 'fail'. This may seem basic but if students do not feel as though they can verbalise their initial responses to a question without ridicule or embarrassment, they will struggle to formulate anything more than the stereotypical 'I don't know what to write'. In order to avoid this, allowing students to feel comfortable in the classroom must be a teacher's number one priority.

The subjective nature of discussion and debate in English is what drives many students (and adults) to love the subject in the first place. The idea that 'no answer is ever wrong' in English is not without its problems, however with a well-reasoned and resourced argument, there truly is no wrong answer. Students with the imagination to do so without prompting or scaffolding are few and far between. So where do our ideas come from? How do we formulate them?

We talk.

Oracy and independent thought

Oracy is, in itself, a skill which needs to be modelled. Allowing students to debate the extent to which Hyde is a manifestation of Jekyll's fears about human nature and, therefore, himself in *The Strange Case of Dr Jekyll and Mr Hyde* demands the prerequisite knowledge of Hyde's conception and creation, his actions, description, Victorian society, the importance of reputation, science in the 19th century and Stevenson's own background. To ask students to hold this information in their working memory and cherry pick elements to formulate a coherent response in front of their peers is a monumental task for some.

To simplify the process, it could be useful to break the topic down in to its composite parts. Take one element, such as Victorian society. Discuss the relevance of reputation to a man of Jekyll's stature. Ask open-ended questions such as:

- Why is Jekyll supressed?
- How might someone like Dr Jekyll feel about himself, if society demonises a natural part of his character?
- What drives Jekyll to turn to 'transcendental' science? Why?

An element of preparation regarding vocabulary and question choice, as well as using well known approaches to questioning in order to fully engage students in the discussion, models how they should then engage with the other elements independently.

Students then grapple with another nugget of information – in pairs or small groups – and discuss it. Use research prompts, notes, the text itself and, of course, each other. Introducing the idea of a devil's advocate to the group to challenge their ideas – all through talk. Once they have road tested their own ideas in this way, students have had a taste of success and can then feel their ideas – their concepts – have already been through a form of editing before pen ever meets paper.

Class-wide feedback and discussion of thoughts can now begin. It is often most useful to model the way in which those ideas should then be physically drafted on the page. Visualisers and whiteboard spider diagrams that explicitly show the link between one facet and another can begin to form schemas of concepts – visually modelling the links between Hyde's birth and science in the 19th century, for example. By taking student ideas word for word as they deliver them, their confidence and concepts begin to grow, learning from one another and continuing to practise constructing conceptualised thought as they go.

Reconstructing conceptualised thoughts

Students can have an array of thoughts and ideas, and deciding which of them is most perceptive, most unique, most thought-provoking can be a daunting task. A simple approach can be to start at the end. What is it that students want to say? A one sentence response to the question is a great place to start. Taking their spider diagram from the discussion task, students choose one element they feel they can write the most about that is best resourced and they are most comfortable with. Then simplify this in to a one sentence answer.

Question: Hyde is a manifestation of Jekyll's fears about human nature and, therefore, himself. To what extent do you agree?

Conceptualised introduction: Through the development of Jekyll's character, fears around being exposed as an unnatural and altogether disreputable gentleman are encapsulated in the animalistic and paranoid Hyde – a crude callous creation borne out of pure evil who would be uneasily familiar to readers of the 19th century shilling shocker.

With vocabulary rich, knowledge driven talk and a safe environment in which to debate, conceptualised responses can become every bit as multifaceted as the interpretations of texts they are founded in.

You can follow Avril on Twitter @avs1289.

References

Caviglioli, O. and Goodwin, D. (2021) *Organising Ideas*. Rugby: ResearchED Rugby 2021.

Enser, Z. and Enser, M. (2020) *Fiorella & Mayer's Generative Learning in Action*. Woodbridge: John Catt Educational.

CLOSING THOUGHTS

At the time of writing the book, the teaching profession has probably gone through one of its most challenging periods in a long time. The pressure on teachers and school leaders throughout the last two academic years has been unprecedented. What has been apparent throughout this period is that the profession continues to demonstrate resilience and an unwavering determination to support every child to be the best they can be. After all, as teachers, our job is to help build the character and leadership skills of every pupil so that they can become globally aware citizens.

Over the years, while the core purpose of being a teacher has never changed, the conditions that teachers of the past, present and future have, and this is something we have wrestled with. Without the continued passion and determination from practising teachers and leaders to challenge some of the funky pedagogy and unforgivable workload pressures, we risk losing great practitioners. More importantly, we risk losing greater practitioners in the future too. For teachers to be able to find the 'sweet spot' in their classrooms, school leaders need to be able to 'clear the path' and support them in their day-to-day practice.

Throughout the book, there is a recurring theme that teaching with precision is possible if the right conditions exist to enable teachers to do so. Equally, teaching is an evolving and ever-changing role and teachers are always learning how to continually improve for the benefit of their pupils. I hope that by sharing my own experiences, unpicking some of the research, and providing a glimpse through the keyhole of other teachers' classrooms, this book will provide you with the core principles and practical strategies to use in your own classroom.